# You're not
# crazy–
# You're
# grieving

6 Steps for Surviving Loss

# You're not crazy– You're grieving

## 6 Steps for Surviving Loss

ALAN D. WOLFELT, PH.D.

Companion
PRESS

Fort Collins, Colorado
An imprint of the Center for Loss and Life Transition

Companion Press is an imprint of the
Center for Loss and Life Transition
3735 Broken Bow Road
Fort Collins, Colorado 80526

Printed in the United States of America

30   29   28   27   26   25   24   23           5   4   3   2   1

ISBN: 9781617223228

# In Gratitude

*I offer my overwhelming appreciation to the thousands*
*of people who have taught me about their grief,*
*all of whose experiences are reflected in this book.*

Companion
PRESS

Companion Press is dedicated to the education
and support of both the bereaved and bereavement caregivers.
We believe that those who companion the bereaved by walking
with them as they journey in grief have a wondrous opportunity:
to help others embrace and grow through grief—
and to lead fuller, more deeply-lived lives themselves
because of this important ministry.

For a complete catalog and ordering information, write or call:

Companion Press
The Center for Loss and Life Transition
3735 Broken Bow Road
Fort Collins, CO 80526
(970) 226-6050
www.centerforloss.com

# Contents

# Introduction

Someone you love died, and you are struggling.

You may feel torn up. Strange. Restless. Moody. Overwhelmed. Disconnected from reality.

And if you picked up this particular book, you probably feel like you're going crazy.

I have been a grief counselor and educator for more than forty years, and that is the most common way in which people describe their early grief to me.

They say:

"I feel like I'm going crazy."
"I feel like I'm losing my mind."
"I'm losing it."
"I'm feeling unhinged."
"I've lost my marbles."

Then they ask me:

"*Am* I going crazy?"

Let me assure you straight off: It is normal to feel crazy after a significant loss.

But you're actually *not* going crazy in the way you may think.

What you're doing is grieving.

# A Survival Guide

This book is a survival guide for the early weeks and months after a life-changing loss.

It has been my honor to write many books about the normal and necessary process of grief, but this is the first one in which I've focused on the early weeks, months, and sometimes, depending on the nature of the loss, years of intense grief.

I know that it's a difficult time to survive.

Right now, you may feel overwhelmed. You may not yet be able to see how you can possibly go on. It is OK to feel this way for the time being. It is normal to feel shocked, lost, and sorrowful.

But I promise you: You can survive this. It won't always be this painful. You can come out of the dark and into the light.

In the meantime, I hope you will lean on this book to help you survive your most challeging days.

## Crazy Is Normal

Again, I remind you, it is normal to feel crazy after a shattering loss.

What I want you to consider is that it is actually the *loss* that's not normal. This loss came along uninvited and turned your life upside-down.

Human beings are born to live and love. That's why we are here. When a life ends, we're simply not prepared. We *can't be* fully prepared, even when a death is anticipated. Why? Because it's human nature to want and expect life and love to continue. We're just not made to easily welcome death into our daily lives.

Yes, it's true that death is also normal and natural. But still, love is the foundational experience of our lives. And when we

# WHAT I MEAN BY CRAZY

**"A heart broken as wide and deep as mine was...
At first, I wasn't so sure it could be put back together again."**

The term "crazy" is no longer considered acceptable in mental-health circles. Rightfully so. It stigmatizes mental-health issues and places blame and shame on those who suffer from mental-health challenges.

So when it came time for me to write this book, I had a conundrum. "Crazy" is in fact the term I've heard grieving people use most often to describe their own early-grief experiences of shock, disorientation, protest emotions, and more. Actually, they almost always use the word "crazy" to collectively label all their early-grief symptoms. Have you described your own grief responses as crazy?

The word "crazy" comes to us from the 14th century Germanic word *crasen*, which meant "to shatter, crush, break into pieces." Before that existed the Old Norse *krasa*, which also meant "to shatter."

If you pick up an old piece of fine china, you might see a web of fine lines on its surface. This is called "crazing." The glaze, normally transparent and invisible, has shattered into tiny sections.

Early grief is equally shattering. It crushes us and breaks us into a million pieces. This experience tends to make us feel, well, crazed for a while—for weeks, months, and sometimes even years.

So I decided to use the term "crazy" in this book title after all. I agree it's not an appropriate term for mental illness because it carries too much baggage and stigma. But grief, which is not an illness, often feels crazy in the truest sense of the word because it can shatter you, crush you, and make you feel like you've broken into pieces.

experience the death of a loving relationship, we often feel like we are going crazy.

Of course we do.

## Grief Is Normal

A few paragraphs ago I said that it is loss that isn't normal—not our response to loss. That is because we as human beings are built to become attached to people and things. In other words, attachment is our normal state. Anything that breaks up those attachments feels abnormal, at least in the beginning. This includes the most profound separator—death.

So, grief is our normal response to the abnormal experience of loss.

What is grief? It's everything we feel and think inside ourselves after someone dies.

In the early weeks and months, those grief feelings and thoughts tend to be chaotic and surreal. They can make us feel crazy. But actually, they're normal.

The pain, too, is normal. It feels terrible, unbearable, unsurvivable. Yet the pain also makes sense because being shattered and broken is a painful experience. There's no way around that.

Another very important thing to understand about grief is that it's love. Love and grief are two sides of the same coin. Grief is what love feels like when we are separated in some way from the object of our love. And if love is normal—which of course it is!—then grief is normal, too.

Here I must also note that not all attachments are loving. If your relationship with the person you're grieving was more complicated or ambivalent, your grief will likely be more complicated as well. In general, grief always mirrors all the feelings and dynamics associated with the relationship—not just the love, though love and attachment are always the anchor points.

Mourning is normal as well. Mourning means expressing our inner feelings and thoughts of grief. It's getting our inside grief outside of ourselves. When we cry, we're mourning. When we talk to other people about our loss, we're mourning.

Over time, mourning is what glues our shattered pieces back together. Mourning helps us heal.

## One Second at a Time

How do we survive great loss in the early days? We do what you have likely been doing since day one: We take it one second at a time.

That is how you have been surviving so far, right? One day at a time, one minute at a time, sometimes one second at a time.

Earlier I promised that you can survive this. You will not always feel this bad. What makes me so sure of this fact is that I have had the privilege of companioning thousands of grieving people in my career as a grief counselor and educator.

---

### COMPANIONING

Years ago, I developed a grief-counseling model I call "companioning." Companioning means to walk alongside the grieving person—bearing witness, listening, affirming, and learning from them instead of the other way around. I urge you to reach out to grief companions on your journey. On our website, www.centerforloss.com, you can find a list of grief companions I've had the honor of training. (For more information on the companioning philosophy, see Appendix A, page 125.)

---

In the early days of their grief, most of the grieving people I've been honored to learn from told me they felt like they were going crazy. Many of them were not at all sure that they would be able to survive.

But they did. Those survivors often reach out to me years later. "I'm a different person now," they report. "My grief is not completely gone and never will be, but it's become part of me. I'm doing well. I'm grateful to be alive."

They were once where you may be now. There is a bridge from here to there, and it is called hope.

Hope is an expectation of a good that is yet to be. You can be crazy with grief and still hold onto hope. They are not mutually exclusive. In fact, I want you to think of them as a pair, like a lock and a key. Grief and hope belong together. In addition to the one-second-at-a-time philosophy, this is another secret to surviving loss.

Stop and inhale deeply and slowly. Exhale deeply and slowly. Do it again. You have survived a few more seconds. You are alive and figuring out how to keep living. It is my sincere hope that this book can be your helpful companion as you walk the bridge from here to there.

In the meantime, keep breathing, and trust that there is still good in store for you. And strive to be OK with taking it slowly. In grief, there are no rewards for speed.

## How to Use This Book

This book introduces six steps to surviving the initial weeks and months of loss. They're a kind of a "how-to" of not only making it through your early grief but also setting out on a healthy path toward longer-term healing.

Step 1: Know that your intense, unique grief is normal and necessary.

Step 2: Do whatever you need to do to feel safe and comforted.

Step 3: Acknowledge the illusion of control.

Step 4: Tell the story.

Step 5: Embrace your spirituality.

Step 6: Step toward living even as you grieve.

The six steps are based on my six central reconciliation needs of mourning, which I developed and have strongly advocated for throughout my career as a grief counselor and death educator. However, because of the uniqueness of early grief, I created these six steps to support you in the first weeks and months after a significant loss. (For more information on the six needs of mourning, please see Appendix B, page 127.)

As you read this book, you'll find that the six steps don't prescribe how your grief "should" be, however. You and you alone are the expert of your own grief. In fact, that's a theme in this book. When it comes to grief advice and how to live with your grief, you get to decide what works for you and what doesn't. You are in charge.

The steps invite you to start from your own authentic grief and explore, take ownership of, and express your experiences fully.

The six steps are listed in order, 1 through 6, but they're not really sequential. Yes, Steps 1 and 2 tend to be more important to work on first, and Step 6 is typically more pertinent later on, but you can be engaging with any, some, or all of the steps at any time in your early grief.

What's more, the steps are *not* a checklist. You can't check off Step 2, for example, and assume you are "done" with it. Fear and anxiety about your loss may come up for you on and off for months, sometimes years. So, you may find that you need to return to Step 2 occasionally to work on feeling safe and secure again. This is totally normal.

As you read through the discussions of the six steps in the chapters to come, you may find that you're not ready to explore some of them. That's OK. Go at your own pace, and revisit the book in a month or two. As I said earlier, you are the expert of your own grief. I trust you will know when you are ready. You get to decide.

## The Grief Stories

Before I began writing this book, I sent out a request to my email list, including both people I've counseled over the years and participants from my grief-caregiver trainings. I asked them to tell me about their experiences with feeling crazy after a loss. In response, I received a number of anecdotes and reflections on their experiences.

I have included bits and pieces of many of their responses in the chapters to come. You'll find them in the quotations in the gray boxes. I hope they will remind you that what you may be feeling and experiencing is normal. You are not alone.

You see, feeling crazy after the death of a loved one can make you feel isolated. Because your going-crazy thoughts and feelings mostly happen invisibly, inside of you, you may feel like you are all alone, disconnected from the world around you.

Hopefully when you see the real-life anecdotes in this book, or you talk to other people about their experiences with feeling crazy in grief, you realize that you're actually not at all alone.

Feeling crazy in early grief happens to almost everyone. The grieving people whose experiences appear in this book walk beside you. My hope is that their stories affirm yours.

## The Power of Intention

Before we dive into the six steps, it's important for me to share that I'm a big believer in the power of intention. Regularly devoting time and attention to thinking about where you want your life to go can shape your future for the better.

If you allow yourself to spend just a few minutes each day considering your longer-term hopes and dreams, you're more likely to forge a path that moves you toward them.

> "At one point, I realized I had to make a choice. I saw myself at a crossroads. For a while I thought I'd just take the road to stop living. But then I decided that would not serve his memory well. So, I decided to focus on the other road and live as best I could until I die."

So, what are your hopes and dreams for your future? Right now, you may not know. Perhaps you can borrow some hope from others for a while until you can generate some of your own. When you are ready, ask yourself: How do I hope to be spending my time? Where do I want to be living? Who do I want to be sharing my time with? What do I wish for my remaining precious days her on earth to be like?

Earlier I said that hope is a bridge. Intention focuses and strengthens hope. I suggest that you spend a few minutes each morning thinking about your hopes and intentions. You might have intentions for the day, for the week, for the month.

Eventually, you might also have intentions for next year and even further.

For purposes of this book and your grief work, try coming up with intentions that are centered around being self-compassionate as well as your relationships with others. Practical tasks that belong on a to-do list are also intentions of a sort. However, when it comes to intentions in grief, I want you to focus on your emotional, social, and spiritual health.

Once you choose them and put them into words, your intentions can help guide you through your crazy time. They can be your North Star. Write them down here and in the chapters to come. Also, if you like to put pen to paper, consider starting a journal. As your intentions evolve and change, which they naturally will, you can keep adjusting them, revising them, writing them down, and referring to them regularly.

Today I intend to: _____

_____

_____

_____

_____

_____

This week I intend to: _____

_____

_____

_____

_____

_____

_____

_____

This year I intend to: _____

_____

_____

_____

_____

_____

_____

In my future life, I intend to: _____

_____

_____

_____

_____

_____

_____

## THINGS TO REMEMBER

In grief, crazy is normal.

Grief is love.

Mourning helps you heal.

Grief and hope belong together.

There are no rewards for speed.

You get to decide.

# Know that Your Intense, Unique Grief is Normal and Necessary

> **"My whole sense of reality became fully distorted. The laws of the universe felt broken, and I was unsure if the sun was going to rise. I remained that way for months."**
>
> ---
>
> "I was at the mall trying to shop and then I spent an hour looking for my car only to remember a friend had dropped me off there. That is the day I thought I was losing it and decided to seek some support. I'm so glad I did because I literally thought I was going crazy."

Grief is arguably the hardest thing we as humans ever experience. It can also feel like the craziest.

I sometimes call the first weeks and months of grief an Alice in Wonderland time because they can seem so surreal.

Everything is suddenly, completely different and strange. It's this strangeness—as well as the intensity that often accompanies it—that makes people in early grief feel crazy. Their thoughts, feelings, behaviors, and encounters are so bizarre and unlike what they were before the loss.

You have probably been living in this crazy new world for a while now. How has it been for you? How have you felt inside? How have you acted? What have you done or not done? How would you describe your most crazy, bewildering, distressing, head-shaking moments?

No matter what your grief experience has been like so far, I want you to know that it is OK.

Whatever you have thought, whatever you have felt, whatever you have done (or not done), whatever you have said (or not said), it is OK.

You are a human being who has suffered a great loss. What is happening to you is what happens to people when they are shattered—or crazed—by loss. There are no rights and wrongs.

When you're feeling crazy, try taking a moment to remind yourself of the truth of what is happening:

*I am normal. I am grieving.*

*I am normal. I am grieving.*

*I am normal. I am grieving.*

Not only is your crazy grief normal, it is also necessary.

Really? Yes. It's necessary because grief is the process of coming to terms with and integrating your profound, life-changing loss into your ongoing life. You are still alive, so you must grieve.

Grief and mourning are the only way to get from here to there. They're not something you or I or anyone else would ever choose. But they're where you are, and you can only ever start from where you are. Wherever that is for you, that's where I'm trying to meet you in this book. We'll start from where you are.

# Respecting the Uniqueness of Grief

In this chapter we're going to begin talking about many of the typical intense and crazy thoughts and feelings that people experience in the early days, weeks, and months after a painful loss.

I just used the word "typical." It is a truth that if we got all the grieving people in the world together in one room, they would indeed have a lot in common. Their stories and experiences would be similar in many ways.

But at the same time, each grief is unique. Just as human fingerprints look a lot alike, they are also singular. Your life, your love, your relationships, your personality, the circumstances of the death, and many other factors make your grief as unique as your fingerprint.

The same goes for others, of course. Their grief is unique, too. Even people who are grieving the same loss often have very different grief experiences.

As I said in the Introduction, you and only you are the expert of our own unique grief. If your grief has seemed extreme, strange, or outside the bounds of "normal" in any way, it's good to remind yourself that you're not abnormal—you're you.

So be kind to yourself, and give yourself the grace of assuming you are doing the best you can in an overwhelming, life-shattering situation.

Respecting the uniqueness of grief is a basic principle in this book. We don't judge ourselves or others. Instead, we approach all grief experiences with empathy and compassion—including our own.

Loss is challenging enough. Let's not make it more challenging by being critical of our natural human responses to it.

## Intense Early Thoughts and Feelings

The intensity and strangeness of early grief tend to make people feel crazy. Let's talk about some of these powerful experiences and affirm that they are common and normal. Again, the quotes you will find scattered throughout this section are excerpts from real people who chose to share their feeling-crazy grief stories.

Because your grief is unique, however, you get to decide which parts pertain to you and which don't. If something doesn't fit, it's fine to skip over it. As your grief naturally shifts and changes in the months to come, you might find that certain sections that didn't seem pertinent at first may become relevant later on.

### SHOCK AND NUMBNESS

Shock is often an instinctive human reaction to traumatic experiences. It is how our bodies respond in an effort to protect our minds and hearts from shattering new realities.

**"I could not believe what I was looking at.
I thought that if I walked out of the room then walked
back in, this is not what I would see."**

"As we started calling people to let them know,
I kind of just shut down. I didn't eat, feel anything, do anything.
I was just numb."

**"I walked around in what felt like a daze for weeks.
It was almost as if I was outside myself looking in."**

Shock is an anesthetic. It partially numbs us to the crushing pain. Without the initial protection of shock and numbness, we couldn't survive a major loss. Thank goodness for shock!

In the early days after the loss, you may have experienced physical shock symptoms such as lightheadedness, nausea, heart palpitations, and difficulty functioning in your body. Emotional shock symptoms include numbness, confusion, and dissociation. Depending on where you are in your grief journey right now, you may still be experiencing some of these symptoms of shock.

During your period of shock, you may find yourself intensely crying, having angry outbursts, shaking uncontrollably, or even laughing or fainting. You might also experience manic behaviors, such as cleaning out closets or pacing and talking nonstop. Rest assured that these are all normal shock responses.

Unfortunately, some people may try to discourage or judge your shocky behaviors, believing them to be hysterical or out-of-control. They may try to inappropriately quiet and placate you because they themselves would feel more comfortable if you appeared composed.

But the reality is that the early days and weeks after a major loss are often an uncontrollable, crazy time. Trying to control yourself could mean suppressing your instinctive responses to the loss. As long as you're not hurting yourself, someone else, or destroying property, it is OK to feel and act out of control in early grief.

### DISSOCIATION AND SURREALNESS

Dissociation is a feeling of separation or distance from what is happening around you. This is when you feel like you are there but not there. Or, that you are somehow disconnected from experiences that you're right in the middle of.

Dissociation can be an aspect of shock. It may feel strange and even scary sometimes, but it's common and normal.

> **"I went through all the motions,
> but it was like I was disconnected from myself."**
>
> ---
>
> "The pictures of the gathering show a person who looks like me,
> but the smile is just pasted on the shell of who I am."
>
> ---
>
> **"I felt then and still do like I'm in a bubble looking out on the world."**

In early grief, you may also feel a sense of surrealness. Surreal means bizarre, irrational, even make-believe. Your mind can interpret that what is happening can't actually be happening because it is not possible for it to be real.

"It feels like a dream," grievers often say. "I feel like I might wake up and none of this will have happened." That dreamlike aspect of early grief is surrealness. It often feels overwhelming and can be naturally disconcerting, but it happens to almost everyone right after a major loss.

### TROUBLE THINKING

It is almost impossible to think clearly in early grief. Brain fog is common. So are problems with short-term memory. You might have conversations with others but not remember what they said to you. Your mind is blocking. You are hearing but you can't listen well.

In addition, you may feel like you can't get anything done. It is difficult to concentrate long enough to complete tasks. You may struggle with basic daily activities.

As one woman wrote to me, "I felt like I had truly lost my marbles. I prided myself on never having locked my keys in my truck. But within the first few weeks after his death, I managed to do it four times. I couldn't remember basic items I needed at the grocery store. In fact, when I walked into the store, I would completely forget why I was even there."

**"I felt like my brain was in a fog."**

"I couldn't work for a year. This caused a lot of friction in my house."

**"I could remember something from ten years ago, but I couldn't remember what I did just a few days ago. My short-term memory seemed to vanish."**

Be patient and kind with yourself if your brain doesn't seem to be working well. It is completely normal. Avoid taking on any cognitively challenging tasks right now when possible. And ask for help when you need it.

## TIME DISTORTION

As human beings, we are creatures of habit. We move through our days and lives with the comforting, predictable structure of routines. So when our routines are thrown into disarray by a death, we tend to get disoriented to the passage of time.

In early grief, often time seems to race by. On other days, it crawls. You may not be able to keep track of what day it is. You may find yourself uncertain of the month or season.

Calculating how much time has elapsed since the death or funeral may feel impossible. Special days such as birthdays or holidays might escape your notice or pass by in a blur.

> **"I was never grounded in time. If you would have stopped me in the hallway and asked me the date, I would have gotten the month wrong."**
>
> ---
>
> "I had no sense of time. I sum up the last year of my life as the longest and the shortest year, which is a strange feeling."
>
> ---
>
> **"Time seemed to be moving at warp speed around me as I was stationary in my grief."**

## SEARCHING AND YEARNING

After someone you love dies, it is normal to look for them or expect them to reappear. In fact, it's one of the most common things people tell me in early grief. Every time you hear your front door or garage door open, your breath might catch, and you might think, "There they are!" This searching behavior is a sign that your mind is trying to process the reality of the death. It can also make you feel crazy because while you *know* that they have died, you don't yet *fully know*.

> **"I kept hoping that the doorbell would ring and he would be at the door. When I watched television, I looked through the sliding door and the large bay window hoping to see him."**

The intense yearning of early grief is similar. You want the person who died back. You miss them intensely. You yearn for them to be present again. The yearning can make you feel crazy because once again, you know it's impossible for them to return, but you desperately want it anyway. Yearning is painful and normal.

## INSOMNIA

Among the most common physical responses to loss is trouble with sleeping. You may have difficulty falling asleep. Perhaps even more commonly, you might be waking up during the night or early morning and having trouble getting back to sleep. The problem with insomnia is that when you're grieving, your body needs *more* rest than usual, not less.

> **"For the first week after his death, I probably had a total of five hours of sleep. I was afraid that falling asleep would mean waking up from a nightmare that was actually true."**
>
> ---
>
> "I just wanted to sleep, but as soon as I got close to lying down, I had a wave of fear and intense sadness. I often found myself standing by my bed, wanting to sleep but not wanting the minutes of pain that preceded sleep."

If you think about it, sleeping is a primary way in which we routinely release control. But when someone in our life dies, we feel a loss of control, and we don't like it. Subconsciously, you may not want to lose any more control by sleeping.

The need to stay awake can also relate to the fear of additional losses. If you stay awake and vigilant, you may think you can somehow help prevent more loss. Some grieving people have even taught me that they stay awake hoping to not miss the person who died in case they return or offer a sign.

All of these sleep-depriving rationales—whether they're conscious or subconscious—are normal and understandable. But you also absolutely need sleep. Not sleeping is bad for your body and can quickly have a deteriorating effect on your emotional and mental health. You probably feel especially crazy if you're not getting enough sleep. So if you're not sleeping well, please check out the suggestions on page 42 and follow through.

## FATIGUE

In general, you might be finding yourself tiring more quickly—sometimes even at the start of the day. You might wake up feeling fatigued.

This is called the lethargy of grief. It might seem crazy to feel so tired, especially when you're not doing anything strenuous. However, it's a natural mechanism intended to slow you down and encourage you to get extra rest and care for your body, mind, and soul.

> **"I do manage the daily tasks and errands, but I still feel exhausted all the time."**
>
> "It takes all of my energy just to get up and take a shower."
>
> **"Even when I sleep I don't feel like I reach deep-sleep. I find I have to rest several times per day."**

Whenever possible, lay your body down for twenty minutes a few times a day. Sleep if you can sleep, but simply rest if you can't. Put on some soothing music or watch a lighthearted TV show—anything that helps you relax.

And don't expect too much of yourself. If you are not getting anything done because you're too tired, it's OK. If you need help getting essential tasks taken care of, ask for it.

## Self-Focus—It's All About You

As an adult, you probably have lots of responsibilities in life. You might have family members to care for, households to run, pets to take care of, jobs to do, financial obligations to stay on top of, volunteer roles to fulfill, and much more.

But now, in early grief, you might be finding that it is all you can do to take care of your own basic needs hour by hour, day by day. You might not want to listen to other people's problems. You might not have the energy to attend to all the needs of your children, other family members, friends, or colleagues. You may feel dumbfounded that the world around you is still turning while your life is at a complete standstill.

> **"I had a difficult time in social engagements because
> I wanted to share deeply about how I felt.
> My friends got impatient with me and drifted away.
> I think I overwhelmed them with my weeping."**

> "How could the world keep going while she is dead?
> How could people laugh and talk as if nothing happened?"

> **"I love my family and friends, but I didn't feel like I had
> the energy to be available to them."**

The compulsion to focus only on your own thoughts and feelings doesn't mean you're going crazy. What it does mean is that you need to take care of yourself right now! Your mind and spirit are directing your attention away from others and toward yourself because you need this self-focus to begin the process of integrating your grief.

You are not being selfish. You are being human.

Of course, if you're a primary caregiver for children, elderly parents, pets, or others, and your need to focus on yourself right now is making it impossible for you to provide them with appropriate care, it's also essential that you solicit extra help. Don't feel bad if you're a grieving caregiver who needs to step away from some of your caregiving responsibilities for a while. You need and deserve respite and intensive care at the moment, so it's perfectly understandable to ask others for help.

As we're always told when we're flying, in case of an airplane emergency, put on your own mask first. You can't help others if you're not functioning yourself.

## Acknowledging the Reality of What Happened

The crazily intense and surreal thoughts, feelings, and behaviors in the very early days after a major loss mostly have to do with one super-challenging need of mourning: acknowledging the reality of the death.

A few pages ago I said that it is not grief that's abnormal, it is loss that's abnormal. But still, your mind and heart have to find ways to understand and eventually accept it. Notice that I said "eventually." That is because fully, deeply acknowledging the new reality takes time—often months, sometimes years.

In the meantime, whenever you are confronted with thoughts and reminders of the death, your mind says, "What? This can't be!" And that's when the crazy-intense grief symptoms we've been going over in this chapter come up. You experience shock, dissociation, time distortion. You may feel like you're being hysterical. You might not be able to think or sleep. You may experience a level of fatigue beyond anything you've ever felt before.

You might think of these symptoms like aches and pains caused by the cognitive grief work your mind is doing. Yes, work. Acknowledging the death of someone close to you is difficult work for your brain.

I don't think we're born being able to easily grasp death. It is instinctive to love, and it is instinctive to grieve when we're separated from the people we love. But it is not instinctive or innate to think, "Oh, it's just death. One minute alive, the next dead. It's just forever. It's natural. It's fine."

Depending on how long ago the person you love died, you are probably coming to terms with the death cognitively. That is, in your head you know and believe that the person is dead.

If you were able to see and spend time with the body after the death, acknowledging the reality often happens a little more readily. It's still hard work—don't get me wrong. But seeing and touching the body that gave form to the precious person who died can help your mind understand the fact of the death. I know that this isn't always possible or appropriate. So if you didn't see or spend time with the body, don't shame yourself. Talking openly about the death and seeking answers to any lingering questions you might have can also help satisfy your mind.

As your mind more deeply "believes" the reality, your shock and numbness start to soften. Any dissociation and time distortion also begin to lessen. You also become less likely to think that the person who died might walk through your door or show up in a crowd.

In the longer run, the need to acknowledge the reality of the death gets passed from head to heart. I often say that you can understand something at the head level but not yet have absorbed it at the heart level. Full heart understanding involves integration of the reality of the death emotionally and spiritually. This takes more effort and time—sometimes even years.

We'll talk more about heart understanding in Step 6. For now, I just want you to remember that your crazy-intense initial grief responses often have a lot to do with the need to cognitively acknowledge the reality of what happened. Your brain is having a hard time understanding and coming to terms with it. That is normal.

## Acknowledging the Pain

There is acknowledging the reality of what happened, and then there is dealing with the pain that naturally arises from that reality.

In the early days, shock protects you from some of the pain. For your mind and body, numbness and dissociation are forms of pain management. Thank goodness for these natural anesthetics.

But still, some of the pain naturally hit you right away. And the pain keeps seeping in every time you think about the death. Even with the protection of shock, you may have experienced moments in the very early days when the pain took your breath away and dropped you to your knees.

Depending on where you are in your grief journey, this might still be happening. You might feel like you are completely immersed in pain.

I know that the pain of grief can feel unbearable, especially when you're not yet accustomed to it. Plus, it can contribute to your feelings of going crazy. How on earth are you supposed to live and function while this pain is going on?

After all, when we experience physical pain, we are used to going to the doctor or pharmacy to get pain relief. There are entire industries and professions devoted to relieving bodily pain. We're not *expected* to suffer.

Yet grief comes along, and we are supposed to just take the pain day after day after day?

First, I want to affirm that you are right—the pain seems unbearable. It is, I believe, among the worst experiences of our lives here on earth.

Second, I want to assure you that your pain will ease over time.

Third, I want you to know that the steps in this book are pain relief for the emotional and spiritual suffering of grief. They can help make your pain more bearable right now.

And fourth, I want you to hold onto the idea that the pain of your grief is your love for the person who died. The discussions in the chapters to come will help you consider that. Because the truth is that the pain is not your enemy—it is actually your friend. And embracing it is a way of healing as well as continuing to love the person who died.

I realize what I'm saying about befriending pain can seem like a challenging—even antagonistic—notion in early grief. But it is a truth.

Your pain is there for a reason. So, for now, I hope you will simply acknowledge that the pain is normal and find ways to soothe it as best you can. Also trust that as we move forward in this book, you will gain a better understanding of its purpose.

## Reset Your Intention

It's time to revisit your grief intentions—those having to do with your emotional, social, and spiritual health.

Today I intend to: _____

_____

_____

_____

_____

_____

_____

This week I intend to: _____

_____

_____

_____

_____

_____

_____

_____

_____

This year I intend to: _____

_____

_____

_____

_____

_____

_____

_____

In my future life, I intend to: _____

_____

_____

_____

_____

_____

_____

_____

## THINGS TO REMEMBER

In grief, crazy is normal.

Grief is love.

Grief and hope belong together.

Mourning helps you heal.

You get to decide.

Each grief is unique. Respect that.

Early symptoms of grief are necessary and normal.

Put on your own oxygen mask first.

Your pain is there for a reason.

# Do Whatever You Need to Do to Feel Safe and Comforted

Have you felt stressed, anxious, fearful, agitated, panicked, worried, or uneasy since the death? I'm not sure grief is possible without these feelings. As author C.S. Lewis wrote after his 45-year-old wife died of cancer, "No one ever told me that grief felt so like fear."

Feeling afraid or anxious is not pleasant, and I know it can be terrifying. Still, fear is perfectly normal after someone important to you dies. And if you've been experiencing fear, it could well be part of what is making you feel crazy.

> **"My heart raced with fear. How could I live without her?"**
>
> ---
>
> "I'm an independent, brave, go-forward person.
> But somehow that bravery was whisked away when
> my husband died suddenly. I was so afraid of the
> present and future without him."
>
> ---
>
> **"I had a bad feeling someone else was going to die.
> For months after I became very fearful that more losses
> were going to keep happening."**

As always, understanding helps us navigate difficult experiences. I often say that we can cope with what we know, but we can't cope with what we don't know. So let's take a closer at the fear of grief, and then we'll discuss what you can do to soothe your fears, comfort yourself, and feel better.

## Why We Feel Afraid After Loss

Why is fear so common in the first weeks and months after a death? While fear rarely feels good, there are a number of reasons it makes sense in early grief.

First, the death of someone we love impacts our sense of safety, which arouses our bodies' fight, flight, or freeze systems. Stress chemicals flood our bloodstreams. Our minds and bodies are placed on high alert for the possibility of more danger.

Second, a death often creates numerous practical stressors. In the first weeks, immediate family members have a lot to take care of. People must be notified and funerals planned. Many forms have to be completed. Financial matters must be tended to. Difficult conversations are required. All of these obligations are stressful and compound the natural biochemistry of fear.

Third, death naturally causes existential fear. It makes us worry about how or if we'll survive being shattered. We are forced to confront unanswerable questions about the meaning and purpose of life. We realize how vulnerable we are—and how vulnerable other loved ones who are still living may be. Life's cruelty and fleetingness are especially pronounced at this time, and they can feel quite scary.

And fourth, one of our core relationships has been severed. Our relationships often make us feel safe and secure in who we are as individuals. In addition, they ground us as part of a family and a community. The prospect of having to rebuild both our self-identity and sense of security can be overwhelming.

It is no wonder fear and anxiety can be such a big part of the craziness of early grief. Acknowledging that fear is one part of Step 2. The other part is finding ways to soothe that fear. Your capacity to build a well-stocked toolkit of effective soothing strategies will help you survive this time.

## The Biochemistry of Fear

We have evolutionary biology to thank for some of the fear-based symptoms of early grief.

When we are under immediate threat, our ancient fight, flight, or freeze system kicks in. This is the biological wiring that evolved to keep us alive in dangerous situations. Here's a quick lesson:

Imagine I suddenly notice that a predator—a grizzly bear, say— is nearby and approaching me. My brain recognizes "Danger!" and activates my sympathetic nervous system and my adrenocortical system. This sets off a cascade of physical responses. My sympathetic nervous system uses nerve pathways in my body to initiate reactions, while my adrenocortical system releases hormones through the bloodstream.

My brain's amygdalae, two small clusters of cells deep in my temporal lobes that are in charge of emotional processing, interpret what I am seeing as danger and instantly send a distress signal to my hypothalamus. My hypothalamus is my stress command center, in charge of my autonomic nervous system. It reaches out to my adrenal glands, which pump out epinephrine, a.k.a. adrenaline.

My heart rate increases, pushing blood to my muscles, heart, and other vital organs.

My breathing rate speeds up so I can take in more oxygen.

My digestion slows down or stops, because it's not necessary right now.

My blood vessels constrict to channel blood to my muscles.

My pupils dilate so I can see better.

My brain receives the extra oxygen and goes into hyper-alert status.

In short, my body prepares to either stay and fight, freeze in an attempt to "play dead," or run away.

After the initial surge of adrenaline subsides, if I am still seeing that scary grizzly bear, my hypothalamus activates what is known as the HPA (hypothalamic-pituitary-adrenal) axis. This second punch in the one-two punch stress response keeps my body in hyper-alert mode.

My pituitary gland releases a hormone called adrenocorticotropic hormone, or ACTH, which travels to my adrenal glands, prompting them to release cortisol. Cortisol is also called "the stress hormone." It maintains my body's fluid balance and blood pressure and blocks non-essential bodily functions, such as reproductive drive, immunity, and growth.

All of this happens without my conscious awareness or permission. Instead, my body's reaction to danger is subconscious and primal.

The name that we use to describe what my body is feeling after I see the bear is "fear." I see danger, so I feel fear. In other words, fear is what it feels like in my body when my body's primal fight-or-flight-or-freeze system has been activated.

For millennia, fear has kept human beings alive. When we are in true physical danger, it still does. You'd better believe that if I encounter a grizzly bear on my next hike in the northern Rocky Mountains, I'll be grateful for fear.

But now human societies and technologies have evolved to the point that in our daily lives we rarely experience imminent life-or-death situations. We most often experience fear after an incident that's scary and/or emotionally stressful.

Death is scary and stressful emotionally. Death causes fear.

## Recognizing Your Fear

Are you aware that you've been feeling afraid or anxious since the death? It can sometimes be hard to recognize fear and anxiety for what they are, especially if they show up in ways that you don't necessarily associate with fear.

Here are some common fear-based symptoms in early grief:

- Feeling nervous, tense, or restless
- Having a sense of foreboding that something else bad is going to happen
- Faster than normal heart rate

- Faster than normal breathing

- Trembling or shaking

- Being fidgety or jumpy; startling easily

- Fatigue and weakness

- Gastrointestinal troubles

- Racing thoughts

- Repetitive thoughts/worries

- Trouble concentrating

- Trouble sleeping

- Avoiding certain places, people, circumstances

- Over-isolating yourself

If you are regularly experiencing one or more of these symptoms, you're probably struggling with fear and anxiety in early grief. It is common and normal. It is also something that requires your compassionate attention.

## Soothing Your Fear and Anxiety

Let's reiterate: Fear in early grief is normal and understandable.

Still, fear can be a paralyzing, all-consuming experience that prevents you from getting the help and support you need in the short term. And if it goes on intensely for too long, it can also harm your health because stress chemicals cause and worsen disease. Studies show that chronic anxiety weakens our immune systems, causes cardiovascular damage, leads to gastrointestinal trouble, accelerates aging, worsens memory and decision-making, and can cause clinical depression.

## SUICIDAL THOUGHTS AND SAFETY

**"I wanted to be dead. I wasn't suicidal, though.
I just wanted to be dead to those intense, agonizing
feelings of loss, grief, and despair."**

---

"I found myself asking God to take me—
not that I would actually hurt myself, because I wouldn't.
I was just in so much pain.
This is when I knew I needed to ask for help."

---

**"I kept thinking, 'I wouldn't mind
if I didn't wake up tomorrow.'"**

Step 2 is about finding ways to feel safe.

If you're having active thoughts of suicide, you're not safe.

In early grief, it's common to idly question if you want to go on living. You might say or think something on the order of, "It'd be so much easier to not be here" or "I wish I was the one who died." These passing, passive thoughts may feel crazy, but they're normal. However, making plans or taking action to end your own life is not normal or OK.

If your vague thoughts of suicide begin to take on planning and structure, get help immediately. Tell others what you're thinking. Sometimes tunnel vision can temporarily prevent you from seeing choices or the bigger picture. Please choose to go on living as you honor the life and memory of the person who died.

Also important: Unchecked fear tends to get in the way of other mourning work that will help you integrate and move through your early grief.

Basically, fear can throw up a roadblock that stalls and even intensifies your early grief. What this means is that learning how to soothe your fears in healthy ways is an essential daily self-care priority.

The following tips and activities may help ease your fear. Any time you feel anxious, restless, or afraid, give one of them a try. Keep testing out different approaches until you find at least a few that reliably work for you.

As with everything in early grief, there is no right or wrong way to do things. You are the expert of your grief. You get to decide what helps you feel safer, comforted, and as relaxed as possible.

### KEEP LINKING OBJECTS CLOSE

Linking objects are items that belonged to the person who died that you might now like to have around you. Objects such as clothing, books, knick-knacks, jewelry, artwork, and other prized possessions can help you feel physically closer to the person you miss so much. They can also help you feel safer and calmer.

If you like to hold, be near, look at, sleep with, caress, or smell a special belonging of the person who died, you're not at all crazy. You're simply trying to hold on to a tangible, physical connection to the person. The person's body is no longer physically here, but these special items are. And if they help you make it through the naturally scary, anxiety-filled early months of grief, so much the better.

> **"I put on one of his old sweatshirts.
> I lived in that sweatshirt for weeks. It gave me comfort
> and surrounded me with his scent and his presence."**

> "My sister gave me his pillow and his favorite hoodie to hold onto.
> I was surrounded by him in my small world."

> **"I wear my mom's favorite ring all of the time.
> It helps me feel close to her."**

While we're on this topic, I would also suggest that you not rush into giving away the belongings of the person who died. Sometimes people hurry into clearing out all the "stuff" because they think it will help them heal and "move on." But as we've said, grief is necessary. Trying to go around it doesn't work and is not a good idea. What's more, the person's belongings can actually help you engage with the steps in this book. Finally, many grieving people have told me how much they regret having quickly gotten rid of the belongings of the person who died—only to wish months later they had them back.

## CARE FOR YOURSELF

Comfort means being at ease physically and mentally. That can seem all but impossible to achieve in early grief, but in between "doses" of active mourning (see p. 43), I hope you will seek relaxation and respite by caring for yourself as much as possible.

If there was ever a time to indulge yourself with your favorite comforts, it's now. In fact, think of them as survival tactics—not indulgences. Take a nap. Curl up on the sofa with your softest blanket and binge your favorite TV show. Eat your favorite comfort foods. Take a long shower or bath. Meet up with friends at your favorite restaurant, or invite a good friend over for take-out. Ask for hugs. Listen to soothing music. Watch the sunset. Play a game on your phone. Play with your pet. Reread your favorite book.

You get to decide what helps you feel comforted or soothed. Whatever those things are for you, do them often and guilt-free. Do watch out for overusing alcohol and drugs (see p. 45), and take care not to over-isolate. But, otherwise, do what helps you soothe your soul.

"What if I don't feel like doing anything?" you might ask. This is common in early grief. It is normal to have an inability to experience joy for a period of time after experiencing significant loss in your life. There is even a term for it called "anhedonia." It's when nothing feels motivating. Nothing feels pleasurable or makes you content or happy. If you read the ideas above and thought that most of them sounded unappealing, you may be experiencing the normal anhedonia of early grief. Other signs include a lack of interest in things you used to enjoy, such as work, sex, food, etc.

If you feel stuck in anhedonia or your grief is preventing you from taking care of your own basic daily needs, it's time to see your primary-care provider or a grief counselor. While temporary anhedonia is normal in early grief, ongoing anhedonia is a potential sign of clinical depression. Please reach out to get the support you need and deserve.

### SEE A PHYSICIAN AND/OR COUNSELOR

If you are feeling so unwell or crazy that you're having a hard time sleeping, eating, and functioning, it's a good idea to schedule a check-up with your primary-care provider. This would also be a good time to consider seeing a grief counselor or therapist for a few sessions.

I'm not suggesting there is anything wrong with you! I have simply seen time and again that getting a little professional reassurance and support for the normal, intense symptoms of early grief can help you better survive and take steps to understand them.

Your medical doctor can help assure you that any physical symptoms of grief you may be experiencing—heart palpitations, body aches, headaches, trouble sleeping, and more—aren't due to an illness that needs diagnosis and treatment. If you're having any physical concerns that mimic the symptoms/cause of death of the person who died—for example, if you've been having chest discomfort, and your loved one died of a heart attack—your primary-care provider can help ease your mind by ruling out this possibility.

Like seeing a physician, grief counseling is another basic form of self-care. Just a few sessions with a good grief counselor can help assure you that you are not going crazy but actually grieving. They can also help support you while you experience your intense pain. Whatever your most hurtful, scary thoughts and feelings are at the moment, you can share them with your counselor. In fact, openly talking about your struggles in the presence of a compassionate, grief-informed counselor may be the single most effective thing you can do to soothe your fears and other intense feelings in early grief.

I've also noticed that some people think of self-care wellness practices such as yoga, massage, and acupuncture as normal parts of routine physical, emotional, and spiritual maintenance. Other people construe them as overly indulgent or unnecessary. When it comes to caring for yourself when experiencing grief, I encourage you to give them a try if they feel right for you.

## MOVE YOUR BODY

As I previously noted, fear is a primal physical response in the body. Moving your body is an excellent way to reduce the stress chemicals while also increasing the biochemicals that boost feelings of contentment, ease, and happiness, such as dopamine, serotonin, and endorphins.

Light exercise can do wonders for lessening anxiety and enhancing feelings of wellbeing. You can start really small if you are not physically active already. Try walking for ten minutes to start with, then gradually increase the duration. If you don't like walking, choose an activity you enjoy more, such as biking, yoga, shooting hoops, pickleball, or gardening. It can be anything you want. You get to decide.

## MAKE SLEEP A PRIORITY

Good sleep and wellness go hand in hand. Poor sleep, fearful thinking, and feeling crazy do too.

As we've discussed, insomnia is often a normal part of the early grief experience. But if you're not sleeping and incapable of functioning due to exhaustion, it's probably time to get help with your sleep.

See your primary-care provider and explain your sleep challenges. Temporary use of sleep medication or supplements such as melatonin might be wise. You can also try relaxation and sleep apps on your phone, such as Calm and Loona. It is worth continuing the search until you find something that ensures you get adequate sleep.

## GET OUTSIDE

When we are grieving, we need relief from our fear and pain. Today we often turn to technology for distraction when what we really need is the opposite: generous doses of nature. Studies show that time spent outdoors lowers blood pressure, eases depression and anxiety, bolsters the immune system, lessens stress, and even makes us more compassionate.

Engaging with the natural world is a tonic for soothing the fear of early grief. Many people find it is easier to feel relaxed in a calm, beautiful, quiet outdoor setting. Find a few natural places you can go to sit and relax. If you have enough energy, take a gentle walk. Notice what happens to your feelings of fear and anxiety.

---

### DOSING YOUR GRIEF

I often talk about the concept of "dosing" your grief. This means that grief is something that you simply cannot immerse yourself in full-time. You have to experience it in small doses followed by longer breaks in between. While the loss is always present, especially in early grief, you can't focus on it all the time. It's too much.

Instead, active mourning is better thought of as an intermittent thing. You talk about the loss, then you go do something else for a while. You cry, then you stop crying and focus on a self-care activity. You get swallowed by fear for an hour or so, then you go for a walk and feel a little better.

In other words, you encounter your grief, then you escape it. You engage with it, then you disengage for a bit. You do this over and over again one day at a time for many months and sometimes years. This is the normal process of healing.

---

## TRY MEDITATION OR OTHER CALMING ACTIVITIES

Meditation, breathing exercises, yoga, and other mindfulness activities are good techniques to add to your soothing toolkit. Try a class, lesson, or app to help you get started. Many people find that once they learn a simple mindfulness practice that works for them, they're hooked. This often helps them feel healthier and more grounded.

### IF YOUR LOSS WAS TRAUMATIC

The natural stress, anxiety, and fears of early grief are typically more challenging after a traumatic death.

What may be considered a traumatic death varies. Sudden and/or violent deaths are almost always thought of as traumatic. Deaths with uncertain causes, out-of-order deaths (such as the death of a young person), and deaths that happen at the same time as other major life stressors or losses also tend to feel traumatic.

If your loss was traumatic in some way, you may be naturally experiencing heightened fear and anxiety. Post-traumatic stress is real. I use the term "traumatic grief."

If you are experiencing traumatic grief, I urge you to see an experienced grief therapist. You may need more care to get through your early grief than you can give yourself and that your friends and family can offer. Your grief is still normal, but the circumstances of the loss are abnormally challenging. The extra layer of support a grief therapist will provide can make all the difference.

## BE CAREFUL OF ALCOHOL AND DRUG USE

Many people turn to alcohol and drugs to help them feel less anxiety and pain after a major loss. Nobody wants to experience hurt of this magnitude. Looking to numb the pain and fear is understandable.

The problem with using drugs and alcohol to cope with grief, of course, is that they can harm our bodies and are also habit-forming. What's more, when they are relied on too often, they distance us from the reality of our loss and grief. I have seen many times that substance use hindered or complicated healing rather than helped it.

If others express concern about your alcohol or drug use, or if you yourself are wondering if the frequency and/or degree of your substance use are healthy, I urge you to talk to your primary-care provider about it. Cutting back is probably a good idea, and if you are struggling with addiction, getting help right now is the wisest, best thing you can do.

## Spending Time with Loved Ones and Pets

> **"My friends took turns staying with me throughout the first few days and listening to my pain.**
> **They are still helping me visit his grave, memorialize him, and embrace my grief."**

I can't overstate how necessary it is to spend time with people (and, if you have them, pets) who care about you when you're in early grief. You may feel like isolating yourself—closing your bedroom door, crawling into bed, and pulling the covers over your head—but too much isolation is not good for you, especially if you're anxious. Being alone with your thoughts and fears only tends to make them worse.

Studies have proven that spending time with friends and family helps us cope with stress and elevates our mood. Because it lowers cortisol levels, it also improves our cardiovascular health and boosts our immune systems, among other benefits.

I'm not saying that alone time can't also be good and necessary in grief, because it is. The natural fatigue of early grief makes rest and solitude a priority as well. But if your fears are making you feel crazy or your anxiety is so pronounced that it is difficult for you to get through the day, please—reach out to others. Texts, phone calls, and emails can support you at any time of the day or night. And whenever possible, spend time with others in person.

Talking about your fears is certainly an effective way to diminish them. The more you express and explore them, the less power they will have over you. But it also helps to simply spend time in the company of others. It's OK not to talk about your loss all the time if you don't want to or have the energy. Keep in mind the concept of dosing. Just being around friends and family is often enough to reduce anxiety and bolster feelings of wellbeing.

Allowing others to take care of you is also important in Step 2. When friends and family members cook for you, clean for you, run errands for you, and take care of tasks for you, what they're really doing is expressing their love for you. They're also trying to help ensure you feel as safe and comforted as possible. If you are someone who is not used to being taken care of by others, you might need to make a conscious effort to accept their support.

Pets, too, provide solace and support when we're grieving. As pet parents know, their unconditional love is such a comfort. It's hard to feel afraid when a dog is licking your face or a cat is purring in your lap. So by all means, if you're a pet person, turn to your pets for soothing whenever you get the chance.

You need other people (and companion animals, if you have them) to help you. Let them.

## Starting the Habit of Checking in with Yourself

My many years as a grief counselor have taught me that people are often unaware of how they're feeling. They move through life *doing*, but they've never learned to be present to their emotions.

If you are not doing it already, now is a good time to start the habit of checking in with yourself.

First thing each morning, last thing each night, and several times throughout each day, stop whatever it is you are doing and ask yourself, "How am I feeling right now?" Name your feeling(s) and care for yourself accordingly.

If you are feeling anxious, take steps to soothe your anxiety. This chapter has suggestions if you need them.

If you are feeling shocky and are disconnected by this, revisit Step 1.

If you are struggling with your mood or feeling out-of-control and want a little support, take a look at Step 3.

If you are powerfully missing the person who died, try Step 4.

As you get better at recognizing your grief feelings and more experienced at coping with and embracing them, you won't need to refer to this book all the time. You'll know you're not crazy—you're grieving. You'll know what to do and not to do to help yourself survive and eventually thrive.

## Reset Your Intention

It's time to revisit your grief intentions—those having to do with your emotional, social, and spiritual health.

Today I intend to: _____

_____

_____

_____

_____

_____

_____

This week I intend to: _____

_____

_____

_____

_____

_____

_____

_____

_____

This year I intend to: _____

_____

_____

_____

_____

_____

_____

_____

In my future life, I intend to: _____

_____

_____

_____

_____

_____

_____

_____

## THINGS TO REMEMBER

In grief, crazy is normal.

Grief is love.

Mourning helps you heal.

Grief and hope belong together.

There are no rewards for speed.

You get to decide.

Each grief is unique. Respect that.

Early symptoms of grief are necessary and normal.

Put on your own oxygen mask first.

Your pain is there for a reason.

Fear and anxiety are normal in grief.

Finding ways to feel safe and comforted has to be a priority.

Dose your grief.

You need people.

Check in with yourself.

# Acknowledge the Illusion of Control

**"What seems to have changed more than anything else in my own continuing life is that I recognize that I never was in control of the most important things."**

Before the person who was important to you died, your life may have felt "normal." What I mean by that is that you more or less knew what to expect on any given day. You had daily and weekly tasks, routines, schedules. Your life was your life, and you were used to it. The predictability was likely comfortable and reassuring.

But now, the death of someone significant in your life has thrown your thoughts, feelings, and behaviors into disarray. Nothing may feel "normal" right now. Your routines and schedules might be chaotic. You may often find yourself surprised at things you think, say, or do. Small things that you used to take in stride might now throw you off track. Everything may feel strange and off-kilter.

You're not crazy, though—you're grieving. Remember, early grief is a naturally out-of-control time. And it is this loss of control that often makes people feel like they're going crazy.

I know it doesn't feel good to be out of control, though. In the

Introduction I suggested that it is human nature to love and be attached. Well, it is also human nature to set up our lives so that they are, for the most part, predictable. Doing so helps us feel some sense of control.

That is because change and unpredictability stress our minds, bodies, and emotions. Any time we encounter something substantially different, we have to assess potential new dangers and figure out new responses. It's hard work, being in new situations—especially those we don't want to be in. But the more we acknowledge that control is an illusion, the more comfortable we can become with the constant change and unpredictability of life.

Step 3 is about being compassionate with yourself as you go through this naturally out-of-control time. It's also about beginning to acknowledge that we as human beings are not really in control of many essential aspects of our lives. When we work to cultivate more awareness that control is an illusion, we can start living with more ease and joy.

## Saying Hello to the Crazy

People typically wish they could take shortcuts around grief. Almost immediately after a death, there's talk of "saying goodbye," "closure," and "moving on."

The trouble is, that's not at all how it works. We actually have to say hello to all the new experiences of grief before we can even begin to think about "saying goodbye." If you're in early grief, you're still in this hello phase now.

In Step 3, one of the big things we have to say hello to is feeling out of control. Because in early grief, being out of control is normal and necessary. Recognizing and acknowledging this is key.

If you've been feeling the craziness of being out of control or "not yourself," you're actually doing what you need to be doing. "This is crazy," you might think on any given day. Or, "I feel like I'm going crazy." But now that you're reading this book, you can follow those thoughts up with this one: "Oh, I see. The crazy is normal. Hello, crazy."

## Acknowledging Your Helplessness

> "Not being able to yell at the person who killed
> my son made me very angry. I couldn't fix this.
> As a mom I fixed it all, but this I couldn't fix."

Individual human beings are largely helpless when it comes to matters of life and death. This is perhaps the most devastating reality of being human.

We like to pretend otherwise. Especially here in America, we teach the concept of "rugged individualism." It goes something like this: I control my own destiny. I can be and do whatever I want. When things don't go my way, it's my fault because I didn't try hard enough. I can fix everything through effort and will.

Yes, of course—individual effort in life does make a difference—but circumstances beyond our control are always at play. For the most part, we can't control who gets sick. We can't control accidents. We can't control natural disasters. We can't control many financial upheavals. And we can't control what other people do.

You were powerless to prevent the death of the person you love, and now you are helpless in the midst of your early grief. Your thoughts, feelings, and behaviors may seem wildly different from what they normally are, and you are helpless to control them. That's OK. Trust that your grief is doing what it needs to do.

# Denial and Step 3

**"At first in the days after he died, I just kept telling myself that he was in the hospital and would be coming home in a few days."**

In early grief, denial can follow shock and numbness. It takes a while for your mind to understand and process the reality of what has happened. In the meantime, you're living in that bubble of shock and numbness. This is normal.

As the weeks pass, though, you might find yourself moving out of shock and into denial. Denial is a more conscious, active blocking of reality than shock and numbness are. Are you feeling in denial about the death generally or maybe certain aspects of the death?

Once a woman whose son died of suicide shared with me that she chooses to think of him as living a few states away. She's placed him there in her mind and heart because she's living in ongoing denial. It's a way to protect herself somewhat from the reality of what happened as well as her pain.

Denial is a form of attempted control. If you can deny that something has happened, you're controlling your perceived reality. You're not actually changing the reality, however. So while intermittent denial in the first weeks and months can be normal, remaining in denial over the long term will inhibit your healing and ongoing life.

As you move through your early grief, taking baby steps one day at a time out of any denial you may be experiencing and into reality is an essential part of the process. You do this by talking with others about the death and sharing stories of your relationship and your loss.

The more you explain and explore the reality of what happened, the more the denial starts to fade. Visiting the gravesite or other final resting place, looking through photos, going through belongings, and participating in meaningful ceremonies are other helpful activities that can soften denial.

# The Out-of-Control Experiences of Early Grief

People in early grief often feel themselves behaving in what can feel like out-of-control ways. Here are a few of the most common.

## CRYING/SOBBING/SCREAMING

> **"I cried so loudly, moaning from the pain.
> I wept and I wept. The next day, my face was so swollen
> I could barely open my eyes."**

> "I went to sleep with tears on my face, and I woke in the
> morning with tears already on my face."

> "In between work and classes, I cried my eyes out.
> I describe it as wailing."

> **"I would scream and cry for hours. The screams coming
> out of me were a sound I'd never heard before.
> They didn't even sound human."**

Tears in grief are normal, of course, and gentle tears are considered socially acceptable. We expect grieving people to cry, and in return we offer condolences and comfort—up to a point. But when crying seems "out of control," we in the West generally don't know what to do. We often judge loud, messy crying as "hysterical" behavior.

In Eastern cultures, sobbing and wailing (sometimes called "keening") are encouraged and understood as a normal part of grief and mourning. In our culture more broadly, however, sobbing and wailing are often seen as evidence of mental instability—i.e., craziness.

But when you are in early grief, of course you're appropriately unstable! That's the entire point! You are naturally shattered and thus out of control. And it is this very loss of control that allows you to authentically express your strong, primal feelings.

If you have been sobbing, wailing, keening, or screaming in early grief, you're normal. If others around you have been telling you that you need to go somewhere to sob where no one can hear you, don't listen to them. If they suggest you need sedatives, say no. It's our grief-avoidant, emotion-phobic culture that's crazy.

And what if you're not crying? This is also common. Sometimes people ask me, "Why am I not crying? What is wrong with me?" The lack of tears often makes these people think they're crazy— but of course, they're not.

If you're not crying, you might still be experiencing shock and numbness. Or you might not be crying because you are avoiding things that remind you of the significance of your loss. Some people have also taught me they fear if they start crying they may never stop. All these responses are normal in early grief.

Finally, you might not be a crier. It is possible to hurt deeply without crying. If this is the case for you, I encourage you to explore whether you're truly not a crier or you've been socially conditioned not to express emotion because tears are seen as vulnerability and weakness. If it's the latter, this is something you can work on.

## MOODINESS

When someone you love dies, you may feel like you are surviving fairly well one minute and crazy with emotion the next. Sudden mood changes can be a difficult yet normal part of your grief journey. These shifts might be small or dramatic. They can be caused by anything—a familiar place, a song, an insensitive comment, a change in the weather, or nothing at all.

> "I had rage outbursts. Big feelings were unleashed. There were lots of emotions I couldn't hold back."
>
> ---
>
> "I had so many emotions packed into even a single hour. It was exhausting to have such huge questions to ponder, feel such intense feelings of anger, disbelief, confusion, questioning, aloneness..."
>
> ---
>
> "I was extremely irritable. Nothing anyone said to me gave me comfort. I actually just felt like telling people to SHUT UP."

Mood changes can make you feel like you're going crazy because your inappropriate self-expectation may be that you should be constantly progressing from chaos to stability. You might think that you should follow a pattern of continuous "improvement" in grief.

In other words, you may expect yourself to keep feeling better and better as time passes. Or, for one predominant feeling to be "over" when you move on to the next feeling.

The reality is, though, that grief twists and turns like a mountainous trail with a million loops and switchbacks. One minute you might be feeling great and the next horrible. One day you might be feeling sad and the next wildly angry—only to feel deeply sad again the next day.

And in general, grief usually gets worse before it gets better. As the Novocain of shock and numbness wears off and heart understanding grows, the pain often intensifies for a time.

So, if you are having normal ups and down and wild swings, don't be hard on yourself. Instead, practice patience and self-compassion. Allow your moods to come and go without self-judgment. It can be hard to think rationally when your emotions are volatile, but try to remind yourself that your moodiness is normal. All your emotions belong.

## PAIN

Early grief hurts so much, especially when the shock and numbness start to wear off. The hurt is usually in proportion to the level of attachment you had to the person who died. Though many other factors also come into play, in general the stronger the love and the closer the day-to-day relationship, the more painful the grief.

For many people in early grief, the pain feels out of control. It is more powerful than they are. It is like an earthquake, tornado, or tsunami—gigantic, terrible, and crushing.

Earlier, though, I said that the crushing pain is there for a reason.

It's time for me to explain what I mean by that.

In grief, pain has a purpose, just like bodily pain. Pain in your body signals that something is wrong and that care and rest are needed. If your inflamed appendix didn't use pain to alert you to the problem, your appendix would burst, and you might well die. Likewise, if your twisted ankle didn't hurt, you would continue with your normal activities, and you might permanently destroy the joint and surrounding tissues.

Similarly, the pain of your grief signals that something is wrong, and you need care and rest. Loss is a wound, and wounds hurt. Your pain announces your loss. It says, "Acknowledge me! Pay attention to me! Care for me!"

Since the death, your grief pain has probably forced you to slow down. It's caused you to turn inward and really ponder your love for and relationship with the person who died. It's made you think about the meaning of life and death, who you are, what and whom you care about, and what you want to do with the remainder of your days.

Your pain is also directing you to take good care of yourself and accept the care of others. In fact, your pain probably led you to read this book.

Just as a severe physical wound requires intensive care, your severe emotional and spiritual wound also requires your attention. The pain is the primary and essential mechanism that forces you to seek the rest you need and the care you deserve.

While we're at it, let's look at the alternative. What if loss didn't hurt? Imagine if you could fiercely love someone who was living, yet when they died, you experienced no pain. Instead, you just shrugged and moved on. Could that really be love? I don't think so.

The capacity to give and receive love—our greatest gift—is here and now. When the object of our love is gone, there is an after. In the after, our love continues, but it needs to find new ways of being. And adjusting to the after is what hurts.

Your pain is an alarm bell signaling that there is work to be done. It's grief work. It's mourning. The adjusting and healing in the after don't just happen. They take attention, time, effort, and devotion. Just like the love did.

The pain of your early grief may feel crazy, but actually, it is good and true. The more you learn to befriend it, the more you will see that it is there to help you adapt to the new reality and find ways to continue to live and love well in the future.

## Triggers and Griefbursts

**"When a griefburst snuck up on me and knocked me down for the first time, I thought I had totally lost my mind and strength. I felt like I was going backwards in my grief."**

"Sometimes it would be a smell that brought me back to her; other times it would be someone who resembled her. But most of the time it was nothing at all—I would just be driving or watching TV and suddenly become short of breath and tearful. It lasted maybe four seconds yet was very intense and came on suddenly."

You have probably realized that certain things can make your grief ramp up from zero to 60 in a split second. You are going through your day and then *wham*—you are suddenly sobbing or can't breathe or shaking uncontrollably. These experiences can sometimes feel like panic attacks.

I call these sudden, intense moments of grief "griefbursts" because they burst in on you, often without warning. They can be so powerful that they bring you to your knees.

Anything can trigger a griefburst, but it's often a person, place, song, food, smell, photo, TV show, belonging, or another encounter that strongly reminds you of the person who died or your loss. And sometimes it is simply an unconscious, unprompted reaction.

Griefbursts are normal. They tend to happen more often in early grief (especially once the initial period of shock and numbness is fading), but for many people, they continue sporadically forever. They usually only last a few minutes. They're exhausting, and while your body will usually relax quickly, the emotions they bring to the surface can linger. This, too, is normal.

So even though griefbursts are normal, they can be upsetting and disruptive. They can make you feel crazy. If you're afraid that a griefburst might occur in public, or when you go to a certain place or see certain people, you might begin to isolate yourself too much.

The best thing you can do to handle triggers and griefbursts is to prepare in advance. No, you can't prevent or totally control them—remember, control is an illusion. But you can make plans. And you can practice calming techniques ahead of time.

The next time a griefburst bursts in on you, what could you do to help yourself weather the storm? Could you step away from whatever you're doing for a few minutes of privacy? Is there a certain friend you could call—someone who has agreed to be on standby as a listening ear and supporter for just this kind of crisis moment? Maybe you could try deep breathing, a meditation app, journaling, or walking.

If you're somewhere you feel like you can embrace the griefburst when it happens, you may decide in advance that you're going to let it play itself out however it naturally wants to. In other words, you're going to let the grief erupt as it will without trying to control it in any way.

Responding to griefbursts can be a trial-and-error process. The trick is to keep trying expression and calming methods until you find a combination that works for you.

## Self-Identity Changes

> **"I was thrown into a state of chaos.
> I didn't know my identity anymore."**
>
> ---
>
> "Getting to know and understand this 'new me' is a challenge every day. I truly thought I was going crazy because I had to navigate my way through every single day. My old life and routine are such a distant memory. It was like learning to walk again after a debilitating accident."
>
> ---
>
> **"I had invested so much parental energy into my daughter. She helped me know who I was. When she died, I felt like part of me died, too."**

It is not just your life that gets thrown into disarray when someone important to you dies. It is also your sense of who you are.

If someone in your immediate family has died, your family

dynamics and everyone's role in the family has been altered. If a partner has died, you may now feel like half of a whole. If a close friend has died, one of the legs of the stool that is your life is now missing.

You may have gone from being a "wife" or "husband" to a "widow" or "widower." You may have gone from being a "parent" to a "bereaved parent." The way you think of yourself and the way society defines you is changed. This can make you feel crazy to the core.

In addition to relationship changes, death also affects your sense of self as an individual. Who are you in this world? What gives your life meaning? What do you want to do differently looking forward? How will you change as a result of this death?

Working through self-identity changes brought about by loss often takes months and years. It is a process you can develop intentions for but not fully control. So in early grief, I urge you to just be patient with and kind to yourself. One good thing you can do to cope with the immediate shock and pain of self-identity changes as you discover them is to write about them in a journal. Ask yourself: Who am I now? How am I different? What of myself have I lost? How do I feel about this? And who do I want to be in the years to come? If you are not a person that puts pen to paper, then find a trusted friend or counselor to explore these questions with.

You probably won't find answers for quite some time, and that's OK. It is the process of pondering the questions and finding outlets to think through possible answers that's important.

As your life naturally changes, give it time. And give yourself time to first go backward before you go forward. I know it's difficult to sit with your grief. You might well feel miserable and stuck. But some degree of "stuckness" is actually necessary in the early months.

Talking to other people who have had similar losses is also a good way to process self-identity questions and changes. If you've lost a spouse, for example, you may find it helpful to talk to other widows or widowers. You can explore the challenges associated with your unique loss.

A word of warning: I often caution people in early grief to not make any major life changes in the first year or two, if at all possible. If you have no choice but to relocate or take a different job, that's one thing. But if you don't, try to resist any urge you might feel to make quick decisions. It can be tempting to leave a place you associate with the death or to head off in a new life direction in an attempt to outrun the pain. Prematurely replacing a lost relationship with a new one is another common response. But many grieving people who have done these things have later reported to me their regret. Their grief simply followed them. Plus, their lives often became more complicated in ways they didn't intend.

Be patient with yourself and your life as you do the hard work of acknowledging your new reality, getting acquainted with your pain, and remembering. Allow plenty of time to reflect, ponder, and consider different possibilities for your future. Yes, do try new experiences. Experimenting with different ways of being is usually healthy. Simply avoid doing big things you can't undo.

Many people discover that as they work on the need to develop a new self-identity, they ultimately discover some positive aspects of their changing selves. For example, you might find a new confidence in yourself. You might uncover a more caring, kind, and sensitive part of yourself. You may develop an assertive part of your identity that empowers you to go on living even though you continue to feel a deep sense of loss.

But these are usually longer-term discoveries and hard-earned wisdoms. For now, you may be just trying to figure yourself out. That's normal.

## The Crazy Things Others Say and Do

"In the days and weeks following the death of my wife, who had early-onset dementia, I learned that most people do not know how to respond to suicide and can say some pretty stupid and incredibly insensitive things. Even one of my friends told me that my wife's 'greatest gift' to me was to die by suicide, alone and without telling me she was planning it. Are you kidding me? I thought I was losing my mind again."

Sometimes in early grief, other people might make you feel crazy. What you really need is acceptance, affirmation, and nonjudgment. Sadly, some people may imply or outright tell you that your natural grief response is abnormal or wrong in some way.

Platitudes are one way this can happen. You've probably heard some of these gems:

"At least you had him as long as you did."

"I guess God needed her in heaven."

"God wouldn't give you anything more than you can bear."

"He's in a better place."

"Just keep your chin up!"

"Well, you have other children."

"I know exactly how you feel."

"It's time to move on."

"He lived to be 89."

"Time heals all wounds."

"He wouldn't want you to be sad."

"We all have to go sometime."

These and other thought-stopping clichés are harmful because they essentially minimize or try to shut down your normal grief. And when this happens, it might make you feel a little crazy. Why? Because everyone is telling you one thing while your internal reality is telling you the complete opposite.

In addition to saying unempathetic things, the people around you may sometimes *do* hurtful things as well. They might avoid you or pretend nothing's wrong. They might unconsciously reverse roles with you, resulting in you needing to comfort them, instead of the other way around. They may not use the name of the person in your life that has died. They might blame you or put more of a burden on you in some way through their actions. And when such things happen, you might feel like it's your instinctual reaction to what they've done that's wrong—not them.

Just remember that when it comes to grief, it's our culture that's crazy, not you. And that's why people so often say and do hurtful things to grievers—because our culture has generally not taught them loss-related emotional intelligence.

Most of these people are well-intentioned, however, so we

sometimes have to take a deep breath and remind ourselves to have grace. They know not what they do.

## Not Failing at Grief

> **"For several years I struggled with the idea that I was 'failing' at grief. I didn't seem to be 'moving on' or 'getting over it.'"**
>
> ---
>
> "Losing the person you love most in the world can trigger almost unimaginable pain, made worse by self-imposed judgments about 'getting grief right.'"

In early grief, many people think they're doing it wrong. Their thoughts, feelings, and behaviors are so strange, aimless, and out of control that they figure they can't possibly be properly grieving.

Think about the iconic cultural images and examples we have of what early grief is "supposed" to look like. I think of Jackie Kennedy's stoic and dignified presence at her husband's procession. While she was appropriately experiencing shock, many people misunderstood this as the way we as humans should act when we are in grief. Publically staying in control is often seen as the way to be in the face of grief.

Our grief-avoidant culture likes to pretend that grief should be neat and tidy. But remaining stoic, keeping our emotions in check, trying to "get it together"—those expectations are not helpful. If you feel like being emotional, be emotional. If you're wailing or yelling or disoriented or being "hysterical," it's OK. If your thoughts and feelings are chaotic, that's normal.

No matter what you're thinking, feeling, and doing, you are not failing at grief. You are living your truth the best way you know

how. But our culture may well be failing you in supporting
whatever your normal and necessary grief looks and feels like.

## Reset Your Intention

It's time to revisit your grief intentions—those having to do with
your emotional, social, and spiritual health.

Today I intend to: _____

_____

_____

_____

_____

_____

_____

_____


This week I intend to: _____

_____

_____

_____

_____

_____

_____

_____

This year I intend to: _____

_____

_____

_____

_____

_____

_____

_____

In my future life, I intend to: _____

_____

_____

_____

_____

_____

_____

_____

_____

## THINGS TO REMEMBER

In grief, crazy is normal.

Grief is love.

Mourning helps you heal.

Grief and hope belong together.

There are no rewards for speed.

You get to decide.

Each grief is unique. Respect that.

Early symptoms of grief are necessary and normal.

Put on your own oxygen mask first.

Your pain is there for a reason.

Fear and anxiety are normal in grief.

Finding ways to feel safe and comforted has to be a priority.

Dose your grief.

You need people.

Check in with yourself.

You are not in control of life.

Long-term denial harms you.

Being out-of-control in grief is normal.

Griefbursts are normal.

You're in the process of figuring things
out for yourself. It's a long process.

You're not failing at grief.

# Tell Your Story

> **"I found myself needing to tell the story of what happened to her again and again. To family, friends, strangers – her story came pouring out of me."**
>
> ---
>
> "And now I long to hear his name. No one talks much about him anymore. I still long to hear about how he impacted people."

A special person came into your life. You loved them. Many things happened along the way. Then, sadly, they died, leaving you behind and in profound grief.

Is this your story of love and loss? No! It might serve as the roughest, barest summary of your story, but your true story is actually so much fuller and richer than that.

Your story of love and loss contains all the details and complexities of who you are, who the person who died was, what your relationship was like, how you spent time together, who the other people in your shared story were, where you lived, all the memories big and small, good and bad, as well as the story of the death itself. In other words, your story of love and loss is a tapestry.

It can also be a lifeline in the storm of your early grief. Your story is something for you to hold onto and to return to again and again whenever you're feeling lost, adrift, or drowning.

I do understand that remembering is not always comforting. It can also be painful—especially in the early weeks. But even if it doesn't feel like it at first, I am asking you to trust that in addition to fostering hope, remembering and telling the story will help you survive. You can build that bridge from the past to the future, from here to there.

## Going Backward Before You Can Go Forward

Since your loss, some of your well-meaning but misinformed friends and family members have probably been telling you some version of:

"He/she would want you to keep living your life."

"Time heals all wounds."

"Just keep putting one foot in front of the other."

"You need to put the past in the past."

"It's time to move on."

Or, as my mother was repeatedly reminded when my father died four months after their golden wedding anniversary, "You had him for 50 years."

Not only do these oft-repeated clichés diminish your significant and unique loss, they imply that moving forward—in your life and in time—is what will ease your suffering. In other words, they encourage you to keep on keeping on. But the truth is, paradoxically, in grief you have to go backward before you can go forward. There is no "moving on" until you first allow your mind and heart to return to the past as often and as long as they need to.

Our cultural misconception about moving forward in grief stems in part from the concept of the "stages of grief," popularized in 1969 by Elisabeth Kübler-Ross's landmark text, *On Death and Dying*. In this important book, Dr. Kübler-Ross listed the five stages of grief that she saw terminally ill patients experience in the face of their own impending deaths: denial, anger, bargaining, depression, and acceptance. However, she never intended for her five stages to be interpreted as a rigid, linear process to be followed by all mourners.

Grief is definitely not orderly, predictable, or stage-like. Instead, it is more of a "getting lost in the woods" experience. And it is recursive. This means that it twists and switchbacks. It's shaped more like a random, meandering path than a straight line. When it turns back on itself, it tends to cover the same ground more than once. If you're angry for a while, for example, you will probably feel your anger return in fits and spurts in the months to come. In fact, every pronounced feeling in grief usually requires repetition to eventually soften and become reconciled.

Grief is not even a two steps forward, one step backward kind of dance. Instead, it is often a one step forward, two steps in a circle, one step sideways process. It takes lots of time, patience, and, yes, backward motion before forward motion starts to predominate.

## Telling the Story of the Death Itself

Often the first backward-looking part of the story that needs to be explored and revisited in very early grief is the most recent: the death itself. We've reviewed how shock and disbelief are normal and necessary at this time. The death of someone loved often feels unbelievable, even when the death was expected. Our minds and hearts need not only time but also re-encountering the reality of the death over and over before they can begin to comprehend and absorb what happened. Death is just naturally difficult to fully comprehend.

> **"Oh my gosh, I was the worst! I told anyone and everyone! God bless the poor souls who sat next to me on a plane for the first three years."**
>
> ---
>
> "In the beginning the story was the Death Story—all the specific details. I noticed that over time, I recounted less and less of the Death Story and began telling more of the Life Story."

Initially (and maybe still today), you may have found your thoughts returning to the circumstances, moments, and what-ifs of the death day over and over again. This is normal.

It may be normal, but I know it is also painful. Still, over time, the act of expressing those thoughts outside of yourself begins to soften the blow of the reality as well as the pain. Telling the story to compassionate people you feel safe with—people who are nonjudgmental, good listeners—helps you acknowledge and begin to integrate this difficult reality into your life. Talking in groups about what happened also helps. Writing in a journal about what happened helps, too. Being open and transparent on the outside about what you're thinking and feeling on the inside always helps, even when it feels scary or painful at first.

So yes, talking about the death helps heal the acute wound. This is counterintuitive to many people. How can talking about a terrible, painful reality possibly make it better? But here's the thing: You're thinking about the reality anyway. You probably can't stop your mind from returning to it. This is a central feature of your inner grief. But sharing your thoughts outside of yourself—in other words, mourning those same thoughts and feelings—relieves some of the inner pressure. It also slowly begins to help you grow to acknowledge what seems at first like an impossibility.

Mr. Rogers famously said, "Anything that's human is mentionable, and anything that is mentionable can be more manageable. When we can talk about our feelings, they become less overwhelming, less upsetting, and less scary."

Of course, Mr. Rogers was right. So, whenever you find yourself thinking over and over about the facts or circumstances surrounding the death, I encourage you to try expressing those thoughts outside of yourself in some way. In fact, this is a good general principle in grief. Whenever you're thinking or feeling anything about the death, try sharing it outside of yourself somehow. Expression is what eventually generates forward momentum in integrating your loss and helping you heal.

## Actively Exploring Memories

Actively exploring memories that took place throughout the entire timeline of the person's life as well as your relationship with them is one essential way of going backward. This allows you to remember the story so that you can ponder it and retell it to yourself and others.

In very early grief—the first days and weeks—memories often come in a chaotic rush. Photos are gathered for the funeral, and people share stories. It's hard to grasp everything at this time, and many memories can feel especially painful. If you are still in those really early days, you're probably struggling with shock and numbness. You might not feel ready to sit down with a photo album. You may not be able to remember all the stories others are sharing with you. If so, this is normal. Give yourself some time to survive the first weeks before focusing on actively exploring memories.

When you do feel ready, make time to encounter your memories in doses. Set aside half an hour here or an hour there to look through photos and videos. At some point, you may find that putting together photo books and memory boxes is a transformative activity. Going through the person's belongings is another facet of remembering. Writing down anecdotes and biographical information is also an excellent way to explore memories.

## But Remembering Hurts!

"Thinking about my son all day every day consumed me. No matter where I was, who I was with, where I was — my thoughts were of my son. His whole life story played in my head, from the beginning until the day he died."

Yes, it does. Remembering often hurts, especially in the early months. It can feel like rubbing salt into the wound. Why on earth would you want to do that? Have you found yourself avoiding photos, belongings, certain people and places, foods, music, and other things precisely so you can avoid the pain of remembering and getting hit by the terrible reality of the death over and over again?

In the very early days and weeks, it's natural to avoid actively placing yourself in the path of even more memories. Your mind and heart are already struggling to absorb the reality. At the funeral, I hope memories were shared in supportive ways. We know that this is one of the most important functions of ceremony at a time of death. And for some weeks after the funeral, you no doubt had to take care of a lot of paperwork and practical details having to do with the death—plus receive visitors, cards, emails, texts, flowers, food, and more. Conversations with people you haven't yet spoken to about the death invite you to re-encounter the wound of your grief.

So in these early weeks, remembering isn't really optional. During this challenging period, it's OK to do (and not do) whatever you need to do to feel safe and comforted as much as possible.

But a time will come when actively remembering—gathering, cultivating, and lingering over memories—will provide that backward motion you need to eventually pick up healing momentum and be able to move yourself forward. When you might broach this milestone is highly dependent on your personality, the circumstances of the death, additional stresses in your life, your support systems, and more. If you're still mired in shock and numbness at this point, it makes sense to postpone going through photos and belongings until you're ready.

When you are ready, actively remembering helps you:

- encounter your necessary, ongoing pain in doses
- acknowledge the reality of the death in your head and heart
- discover additional meaning in the person's life and your relationship with them
- create your narrative, or story, of the person's life in a way that feels right to you

- feel satisfied that you and others have fully honored the person's life

- begin to select some memories to cherish and comfort you

- potentially make your way toward acceptance and possibly forgiveness of old tensions or wrongs

- integrate the story of the love and loss into who you are and your ongoing life

A key caveat here: If your memories of the person who died include fraught, traumatic, or ambivalent experiences such as abuse (physical, sexual, emotional, financial), violence, difficult relationship dynamics, or other challenging realities, it's usually a good idea to explore them under the guidance of a compassionate grief or trauma counselor. Together the two of you can decide how or if to encounter certain memories. While you're actively remembering, therapeutic techniques like EMDR can be used to help alleviate any distress or post-traumatic grief you feel associated with these memories.

Even if your memories aren't traumatic, however, I understand that sifting through them may still hurt. In fact, over my four decades as a grief counselor and educator, many people have told me that they don't want to immerse themselves in memories because it is too painful. If you've found yourself avoiding looking at photos, watching videos, going through belongings, and/or sharing stories with others, you might need some help initiating yourself into remembering. When you're ready, you can then wade deeper and deeper and eventually feel comfortable surrounding yourself with memories. Having someone to talk to as you look through photos and belongings can make the experience feel more doable and supportive. Sharing memories in a grief support group or with a grief counselor is also helpful to some people.

If you go through photos or belongings, for instance, with a friend, you can cry, tell stories, laugh, wail—do whatever you feel like doing to express your authentic feelings as you remember. There's no wrong way to express your pain or your tender or bittersweet feelings of love. But after a dose of remembering in this manner, move on to doing something else with your friend, and notice how you feel. It is likely that you'll experience a sense of relief and release, much as you do after a good cry. And if you feel some degree of release, you'll probably be a little less reluctant to engage with memories the next time.

On the other hand, you might want to explore memories by yourself, privately. It's fine to do so, but in that case I also want you to make it a point to share some of those memories with others later on. Again, never forget that it's the sharing of your inner grief (this includes memories) that turns your grief into mourning and helps you begin to integrate your story of love and loss into your ongoing life.

## Telling the Story to a Support Group

For some grieving people, grief groups provide invaluable support. In these groups, you can share your unique story in a nonthreatening, safe atmosphere, surrounded by others with the common bond of a loss experience. Grief group members are usually very patient and compassionate with one another. They also understand the need for support long after the death.

In fact, for some mourners, grief support groups form the core of their support systems. If your friends and family lack the capacity to support you well, a good group experience can help fill the gap.

It is also important to keep in mind that those closest to you may understandably grow grief-fatigued in the months to come. Even if you have exceptionally empathetic and supportive friends and family members, you will probably find that grief support-group members can better sustain their focus on your grief (and you on theirs) over the longer term.

"I spent eight weeks in a support group with 12 other people who had lost their spouses. It really helped me to be with others in a similar situation and talk about my loss with people who 'got it.' The group has been my lifeline."

"I was hesitant to join a support group, thinking it would just be depressing. But I found there was no substitute for the common bond of experience. Hearing their stories helped me realize I wasn't really going insane. They touched my heart and helped me feel less alone."

Some grieving people are drawn to joining a support group immediately, while others feel too numb to engage until months or even years have passed. Both responses are normal. Or you may not be a support-group person. Individual counseling might feel better to you. What's more, if your grief is traumatic or complicated—caused by a sudden or violent death, for example— you might find that a general grief support group isn't a good fit.

In general, though, you might think of grief support groups as places where fellow journeyers gather. Each of you has a story to tell, and each of you can be a good listener and supporter of others. Lifelong friends are often made in support groups, and these friendships can help sustain you as well as enrich your life.

If you think a support group might be of help to you, consider reaching out to local hospices, funeral homes, churches, and other agencies. They often retain lists of support groups available in your community.

## Telling the Story to a Grief Counselor

I believe that individual counseling is an excellent addition to any griever's self-care plan. A good grief counselor will help you feel seen, heard, affirmed, and understood as you share the many facets of your story of love and loss. What's more, they will normalize your grief. If you are feeling like you're going crazy or doing grief "wrong," they'll assure you that what you're experiencing is normal. And if it turns out that your experience is complicated, they'll support you in ways you will find helpful.

## Telling the Story of Your Changing Self

"Since suffering a loss of this magnitude, I know I will never be the same. I am not the person I used to be. I don't even know who this new person is. Getting to know and understand this 'new me' is a challenge every day. I truly thought I was going crazy because I had to navigate my way every single day."

When someone significant to us dies, we become different people. The foundation of our lives cracks and shifts. We talked about this in Step 3, but I want to revisit it here because it is also important to tell the story of your changing self as it's happening.

The path from who you were to who you are becoming is a challenging one. You might feel like you're going crazy. It may take a long time before you are able to get a sense of where you're headed. In the meantime, be sure to talk about your self-identity struggles and changes with others who care about you. In other words, tell the story. Be patient with yourself, and don't judge yourself. You're trying to figure things out, and as you do so, you need sounding boards as well as affirmation and encouragement from others.

In Greek mythology, the phoenix is a bird that periodically dies and is reborn. But before it can be reborn, it first spontaneously burns itself to ashes. In other words, it starts over. As you are grieving, think of the phoenix as you go backward or feel stuck.

## Telling the Story of Your Ongoing Love

After the death, you continue to love the person who died. As the dying old man Morrie said in Mitch Albom's bestselling memoir *Tuesdays with Morrie*, "Death ends a life, not a relationship."

So as you tell the story of the death and the life of the person who died, don't forget to also look for opportunities to tell the story of your ongoing love.

In fact, your grief *is* your love now, when the object of your love has gone.

In early grief, finding comfort and sustenance in your continued love for the person who died usually feels like yearning. Perhaps you have been experiencing this. You miss the person so much, and you want them back here with you. It can be a persistent ache. This is painful, but it's also normal. When it happens, try telling the story of what it feels like. In conversation with others, bring up all the hows/whens/whys/wheres/ways in which you miss them.

As time passes, your love will remain strong, but the constant yearning will begin to soften. This will be a sign that you are integrating the reality of the death into your continued life. As this happens, you can continue to cherish your love for the person who died by telling the story of their life. Using their name, sharing anecdotes, celebrating special days associated with the person, holding gatherings in their memory, and honoring them on holidays and special occasions are just a few ways to keep telling the story of their life and your ongoing love for them.

## Reset Your Intention

It's time to revisit your grief intentions—those having to do with your emotional, social, and spiritual health.

Today I intend to: _____

_____

_____

_____

_____

_____

_____

This week I intend to: _____

_____

_____

_____

_____

_____

This year I intend to: _____

_____

_____

_____

_____

_____

_____

_____

In my future life, I intend to: _____

_____

_____

_____

_____

_____

_____

_____

## THINGS TO REMEMBER

In grief, crazy is normal.

Grief is love.

Mourning helps you heal.

Grief and hope belong together.

There are no rewards for speed.

You get to decide.

Each grief is unique. Respect that.

Early symptoms of grief are necessary and normal.

Put on your own oxygen mask first.

Your pain is there for a reason.

Fear and anxiety are normal in grief.

Finding ways to feel safe and comforted has to be a priority.

Dose your grief.

You need people.

Check in with yourself.

You are not in control of life.

Long-term denial harms you.

Being out-of-control in grief is normal.

Griefbursts are normal.

You're in the process of figuring things out for
yourself. It's a long process.

You're not failing at grief.

Your story of love and loss is precious. It needs to be told.

You have to go backward before you can go forward.

Tell the story. Tell the story. Tell the story.

# Embrace Your Spirituality

Your personal belief system can have a tremendous impact on your early and long-term grief experience. You may discover that your religious or spiritual life is deepened, renewed, or changed as a result of your loss. Or you may well find yourself questioning your beliefs as part of your work of mourning.

"Why?" is often a recurring and confounding question after someone you love dies. Have you found yourself asking why?

Why did they have to die? Why now? Why in this way? Why does anyone live and die? Why are we here? I often say "why" questions naturally precede "how" questions. "Why did this happen?" instinctively comes before "How will I survive that it did happen?"

In grief, existential questions tend to naturally arise. It is normal to try to make sense of things, to try to understand. It is normal to wonder about and search for the meaning of life—your life, the life of the person who died, and life in general.

It is also normal to wrestle with the difficult feelings that at times accompany these kinds of thoughts after a death. Anger, sadness, guilt, despair, frustration, and even awe and joy often go hand-in-hand with searching, questioning, and sometimes discovering insights about meaning.

In grief, some why questions are the more practical kind. For example: why did he have a heart attack? Usually that's a question with a physical, knowable answer. If you have answerable questions that keep nagging at you, it is good to try to satisfy your mind by finding the answers.

But most why questions and concerns after a death are more esoteric in nature. In other words, they're spiritual. They're spiritual because they can't be answered with concrete facts and hard sciences. Instead, they have to do with our innate sense that there may be something bigger or greater than us at work in our lives and in the universe. Perhaps, we think, there is something cosmic or divine that we are all a part of in some hard-to-fathom or even unknowable way.

It is important to acknowledge that spirituality and religiosity are not synonymous. In some people's lives they overlap completely —their religious life is their spiritual life. Other people have a rich spiritual life with few or no ties to an organized religion. Still others may not consider themselves "spiritual" but have a philosophy of life they live by.

Obviously, each of us needs to define our own spirituality in the depths of our hearts and minds. Regardless of your beliefs, I believe the following spiritual practices can help you survive the coming months and profoundly enrich the remainder of your days.

## What Do I Mean by Spiritual Practices?

To me, spiritual practices are anything that feeds your soul.

As you're thinking about your own belief systems, consider what helps you do one or more of the following:

- Step away from judgment, control, worry, and conflict.
- Listen to your intuition.
- Experience renewal in solitude.
- Acknowledge the sacredness and privilege of being alive.
- Be your best self.
- Enjoy a sense of wellbeing.
- Feel at peace.
- Give and receive love.
- Feel gratitude and appreciation.
- Smile and laugh.
- Experience playfulness and levity.
- Feel a sense of meaning and purpose.
- Feel connected with others and the natural world.

Any activities that help you experience the outcomes on this list are, for you, spiritual practices. So, if you're tempted to say, "I'm just not a spiritual person," I would respectfully ask you to return to the list above.

## Searching for Answers, and Learning to Live with Uncertainty

In the early weeks of grief, many people struggle with finding reasons to get out of bed in the morning. This is mostly a practical, not spiritual, kind of searching. If that's where you are right now, I encourage you to look to Step 2 for possibilities. Anything that helps you feel safe and comforted is probably also a reason to get out of bed in the morning. If the thought of a cup of your favorite tea or sitting outside in the sun gets you of bed, great. If meeting your best friend for lunch appeals to you, excellent. I urge you to be generously compassionate with yourself by sprinkling your day with activities and incentives that will help you get from one hour to the next.

The more spiritual kind of searching in grief, however, is the main subject of Step 5. There generally aren't easy answers to the grand why questions. Sometimes there aren't answers period. I like to say that instead of pinning down *understanding* in grief, we often have to get more comfortable with *standing under* the mystery. That's one of our chief challenges in grief, in fact—learning to live with not knowing and uncertainty (which also relates to Step 3 and letting go of the illusion of control).

But even if there aren't answers, there is still a lot of value in the search. Simply by exploring your questions and looking for answers, you are allowing yourself to authentically mourn. Ideally, you're talking to other people about your search. You're expressing your feelings about your questions and frustrations. And as you're doing so, you're building and strengthening bonds of friendship and love.

What's more, you might sometimes find glimmers of answers along the way. You may well discover or work toward a way of viewing things that begins to help you make peace with what happened. Any core beliefs you had before the death might be tested, changed, or strengthened. This is all to say that searching for spiritual understanding and meaning is normal and healthy in grief.

## You Get to Decide

One of the main principles I've been emphasizing in this book is that when it comes to how to best survive your early grief, you get to decide. That is also the thing about the unknowable— you and you alone get to decide where your spiritual questions and determinations take you.

Maybe you've already discovered bits of meaning since the death. For example, if people have been kind to you in grief, that is meaningful. If you've acknowledged ways in which your loved one's life made a difference, that is meaningful. If you're discovering things about your changing self, that is meaningful. And if you've been finding reasons to get out of bed in the morning, that is meaningful, too.

Usually, grief's spiritual quest takes a long time to feel settled (and even then, your spirituality may continue to evolve as you learn and grow for the rest of your life). So, in early grief, you are still in the just-getting-started phase. Again, it's really important to work on being OK with uncertainty and questioning. Trying to force answers prematurely is a bad idea because it shuts down a normal and necessary part of your grief—searching for understanding and meaning.

Still, as you search and try to figure things out in your head and your heart, I want you to remember that the answers—even if they're temporary, "just-for-now" answers—are up to you. That means you get to decide for yourself the big spiritual things such as:

*Why events happened as they did.*
Depending on the circumstances of the death, you may or may not find satisfactory answers here. The death might always seem senseless to you. That is a legitimate decision unto itself. But for some grieving people, it's possible to make sense of what happened, even if some of it is guesswork or purely philosophical. Regardless, you get to decide.

*If you believe in some or all or no religious teachings.*

When faced with the death of a loved one, some religious people find themselves angry or questioning their beliefs. Their religions might teach that death is a blessing, for example, because the person who died is now "in a better place," and so being sad equals being unfaithful. Other religious people find themselves rethinking God or changing their minds about their beliefs. And still other people in grief who may not have been religious before a death grow to embrace religion afterward. Any or all of this is normal. You get to decide.

*Where your loved one "is" now.*

Are they in heaven? If so, what is it like for them? Or is their consciousness part of the universe now in some way, as many physicists believe? Or have they simply become part of the constantly renewing earth, as we all will? Again, while some people feel certain in their beliefs about what happens (beyond the physical) after death, it's not an objectively knowable sphere. So, your belief about where your loved one is now is completely up to you.

*If you will forgive.*

If you hold any ill will or grudges against anybody (including the person who died), you get to decide if you will forgive them and to what extent. You certainly don't have to forgive. It's up to you. But I know from my decades of learning from grieving people that many people ultimately do find peace in forgiveness. What's more, it's possible to not forgive some things but to broadly forgive and continue to love a person.

*What the death has brought you.*

Again depending on the circumstances, in the beginning it can often feel like there is nothing good that can possibly come from such a death. But eventually you might grow to feel that some of the ways in which you and your life are changing are indeed positive. This is not to say that you wouldn't immediately trade them back for your loved one if you could.

*How you will live and love the remainder of your days.*
As you've unfortunately experienced, you can't control most matters of life and death. We've talked about the need in grief to relinquish the illusion of control (Step 3). But ultimately you *can* control how you will choose to live your life moving forward. You can't control all your life circumstances, but you do get to decide how you will spend your time and energy. You get to decide how you will nurture your own wellbeing and the wellbeing of others. You get to decide if you will be a spiritual optimist or pessimist. You get to decide if love will be a priority. Yes, you get to decide.

While you're still in early grief, don't worry if your thoughts and feelings about these spiritual questions are chaotic and ever-evolving. That's normal. I often say, "Those who do not search, do not find." So allow yourself to continue the search. And remind yourself that mystery is something to be pondered, not explained.

# But Avoid Carrying Grief

You are indeed in charge of your grief. One crucial caution, though: It's a bad idea to decide to ignore or deny truths about the death and your grief.

Previously, I mentioned a mother who is living in ongoing denial about her son's suicide. I have known other grievers who have chosen not to acknowledge circumstances of the death or difficult aspects of the history of the relationship. Still others have told me that they're choosing to focus only on the positive as they navigate the aftermath of a death. Yes, they're deeply angry and/or sad and/or guilty, but they're choosing to stuff those feelings into a locked vault and throw away the key. They got to decide, and what they decided was to deny truths about the death, the relationship, and/or their own feelings.

The trouble is, denying hard truths in grief and suppressing genuine thoughts and feelings can lead to what I call "carried grief." Carried grief is grief that has not been fully acknowledged and mourned. I refer to this as "unembarked mourning."

It may be locked away, but it's still there. If you embrace and mourn your grief in general but continue to deny certain difficult parts of it, you're still carrying grief.

Carried grief is insidious. It's so dangerous because it's a common, invisible cause of long-term wellness issues that negatively affect quality of life. In my work with grieving people, I have many times found carried grief to be at the root of struggles with anxiety, depression, substance abuse, intimacy, and more. It mutes your divine spark—that essential flame inside you that gives your life meaning and purpose—and it causes many people to in essence die while they are still alive.

If you need help acknowledging and expressing difficult aspects of your grief, I would encourage you to see a grief counselor. They can help you safely unpack your carried grief and find ways to integrate it into your life. The essence of finding meaning in your continued life, living, and loving is to allow yourself to openly and authentically mourn. You don't want to end up living in the shadow of the ghosts of your grief.

# Taking Care of Your Spiritual Self

When I'm counseling someone who's grieving, I always ask them to build spiritual practices into their everyday routines. Even just ten minutes a day devoted to caring for your spirit can have a profound impact on your healing and wellbeing.

So for you, which spiritual practices clear your head, help you feel grounded, and nurture your divine spark? Here's a list of ideas to consider incorporating into your days:

- Go for a walk in nature
- Attend religious or spiritual services
- Sit outdoors somewhere beautiful
- Breathe deeply
- Listen to music that speaks to your soul
- Do something good for your body
- Write in a journal
- Pay attention to your five senses in this moment
- Pray
- Meditate
- Make something
- Spend time with someone who loves you
- Do something that makes you feel hopeful
- Help someone else
- Watch the sun rise or set
- Read a spiritual text
- Practice yoga
- Garden
- Get a massage

- Give a gift
- Read or write poetry
- Express gratitude

You can do a spiritual practice and be mourning at the same time. For example, you can pray about your loss. Or you can spend time talking about the loss with a loved one. Grief and spirit work dosed together are often a particularly powerful combination.

But if you are feeling particularly low or in pain and you need a break from your grief, try spending a few minutes on a spiritual practice that takes your mind and heart off your loss.

# Embracing Mystical Experiences

Since the death, have you had any mystical experiences like the ones in the gray box on the following page? If so, how did they make you feel? And how are you incorporating them into your spiritual understanding of life, death, and meaning?

Mystical experiences are common in grief, and they often give comfort to grieving people. And sometimes, because they fall into the realm of the supernatural, they make some people feel crazy! If you've had mystical experiences having to do with the death or the person who died, you're not alone, and you're not crazy.

It is not unusual for people experiencing grief to feel they're being contacted by the person who died. If the person doesn't show up themselves in some way, such as a dream or fleeting glimpse, then a sign or symbol from them does.

Sometimes this sign comes in the form of a bird or animal. When a cardinal, fox, or butterfly, for example, suddenly appears in your yard or your path, you might take it as a sign from the person who died that they are safe and well.

"One night when I entered the house after work, I immediately smelled my husband's cologne. The scent was very strong, as if he was present in the room. I searched to see what could be the cause. Jim's cologne had been removed from the house long ago. I was unable to find any reason for the scent. It only happened once, but I felt comforted by the experience."

---

"I found the bedside table lamps turned on in the spare bedroom. It was a room I rarely entered. The only reason I noticed is that it was evening and the house was otherwise dark. It baffled me. I have to admit, I felt a bit crazy."

---

"I read somewhere that an ailing son told his family that after he died, he would send them quarters to say hello. They collected 624 quarters. And then I started finding money— in the theater, on the street, in parking lots. On my birthday I found a 2009 dime in a parking lot. My husband died in 2009. I believe he was thinking about me."

Other times the sign comes in the form of smells or sounds, found objects (such as the coins in the story above), or natural phenomenon such as rainbows. Such synchronicities often feel mystical when we are searching for meaning.

There are a few different ways to think about these mystical experiences.

One is that you are in fact receiving real communications from the beyond. The person who died or other spiritual beings are contacting you, usually to give you reassurance that all is well.

Another way to think about these experiences is that mysterious happenings are just that—mysterious. You can't know why these things happen, but you can acknowledge that they do happen.

You can stay open to the mystery without needing to fully understand.

Once again, you get to decide.

You get to decide how to think about your mystical experiences. When other people share their mystical experiences with you, you also get to decide how to understand and respond. Keep in mind, of course, the principle that all grief is unique and valid. There is no wrong or right answer.

I would encourage you, however, to be open-minded and to pay attention to how these experiences make you *feel*. If they make you feel better or curious, then choosing to embrace them is probably a good spiritual self-care decision for you. Pondering and exploring them further can also help you continue to search for meaning.

## Dealing with Dreams and Nightmares

We can think of grief dreams as a subset of mystical experiences. And as with all mystical experiences in grief, you can choose to think of any grief dreams you might have however you would like. As always, you get to decide.

Obviously, pleasant grief dreams are easier to live with than bad dreams or nightmares. Nightmares might make you feel especially crazy. If you're having bad dreams about the death or person who died, I encourage you to talk about the dreams with people who care about you. If your nightmares are recurring and/or often intrude in your waking thoughts and feelings, I encourage you to see a grief counselor to help you explore them. As we've discussed, getting good rest is essential for your body in early grief. If your dreams are preventing you from reaching restorative sleep, it's also a good idea to discuss this issue with your primary-care provider.

> **"I often dreamt of her. Of things that had happened, good times we had together. I also dreamed of experiences that had not happened but I wish had. These dreams made me wake up knowing that, although she was gone, she was always a part my experience here on earth."**
>
> "I would have pleasant dreams of him at times. This sometimes made it difficult waking up because the full reality that he was no longer here would hit me. However, I loved dreaming of him because it helped me feel close to him again."

## Finding Healing in Rituals

There is one additional thing I'd like to say about leaning into your spirituality as a way of surviving your early grief—rituals can help.

What do I mean by rituals? I simply mean actions that we perform in a certain way and in a certain sequence. We perform them for a purpose that has emotional and spiritual meaning and is greater than the sum of its parts.

Rituals don't have to be formal ceremonies, though. In fact, most of them can be brief, informal, and simple.

The ingredients of grief rituals are:

*Intentionality*
Take a few seconds at the beginning of each ritual to speak your intention. In other words, state what you intend to gain or reinforce from the activity. For example, "The purpose of this ritual is to honor and remember what _____ brought to my life."

## Actions

Rituals always involve your body. Moving or using your body in certain ways as you perform a ritual helps integrate your physical, cognitive, emotional, social and spiritual selves. Examples include lighting a candle, holding your body in a certain posture, bowing your head, standing in a certain spot, moving from point A to point B to point C, etc.

## Symbolism

Symbols are significant elements of ritual. Objects important to your story of loss and ongoing love can be powerful touchstones in your cherishing rituals. These are often linking objects but can also be spiritual symbols, flowers, candles, and more.

## Sequence

Rituals have a beginning, middle, and end. The parts of the ritual are usually performed in a certain order because the sequence itself builds meaning and effectiveness.

## Presence

Rituals stand apart from the rest of our days. We don't allow the busy-ness of our lives to intrude on them. Instead, we create a time and place, and we commit to being fully present as we carry out the ritual.

## Heart

Rituals are emotional. In performing grief rituals, we commit to being open to and accepting of whatever emotions arise. We allow ourselves the gift of time and presence to acknowledge, welcome, and feel our feelings, no matter what they are.

## Spirit

The spiritual nature of ritual is what creates the transformative power of the experience. On the surface, we may seem to be carrying out a series of simple, no-big-deal actions. But with the addition of intention, symbolism, sequence, presence, and heart, we are elevating the experience into the realm of the spiritual.

You can combine these seven elements in a million ways to create simple, brief grief rituals to incorporate into your daily life.

One example is what I call the "Ten-Minute Grief Encounter Ritual." Here's how it works:

- First, find a quiet space and center yourself.

- Then set your intention for the ritual on that day. For example, it might be to feel more calm or to appreciate the love you still have for the person who died. It can be anything you want.

- Then, while holding or looking at a symbol of the person who died (such as a photo or article of clothing), name the grief feelings you are having in that moment and acknowledge their normalcy. You might say something like, "I am feeling afraid. Fear is a natural part of grief."

- As you name each new thought and feeling, place your free hand over your heart, pressing gently, then allow your hand to fall to a resting position again.

- If you're someone who prays, you can pray these thoughts and feelings instead as you step through the ritual.

- Continue feeling, naming, and exploring your emotions for five to ten minutes. When the time is up, take a moment to express your gratitude for anything authentic you thought, felt, and acknowledged during the ritual.

- Close with an affirmation that restates the intention you set at the beginning of the ritual but this time as a present truth. For example, "I love _____ (name of person who died). I am capable of grieving and loving and healing all at the same time."

Now that you know what I mean by a simple daily grief ritual, I'm sure you can come up with ideas of your own. If you need more ideas, my book *Grief Day by Day: Simple Everyday Practices to Help Yourself Survive and Thrive* might be of help to you.

The amazing thing about grief rituals is that they naturally facilitate healing. This is especially true when they're done regularly, day in and day out. I urge you to give them a try. I have seen them work effectively many times in the lives and hearts of grieving people. In fact, ritual is so effective in grief that when I meet a griever who is especially struggling, I often recommend additional rituals as well as talk therapy.

If you're someone who's not already comfortable with spiritual practices, the idea of grief rituals might sound a little crazy. But embracing the crazy is what this book is all about, right? You're not really crazy, and grief rituals aren't either.

## Reset Your Intention

It's time to revisit your grief intentions—those having to do with your emotional, social, and spiritual health.

Today I intend to: _____

_____

_____

_____

_____

This week I intend to: _____

_____

_____

_____

_____

_____

This year I intend to: _____

_____

_____

_____

_____

_____

In my future life, I intend to: _____

_____

_____

_____

_____

_____

## THINGS TO REMEMBER

In grief, crazy is normal.

Grief is love.

Mourning helps you heal.

Grief and hope belong together.

There are no rewards for speed.

You get to decide.

Each grief is unique. Respect that.

Early symptoms of grief are necessary and normal.

Put on your own oxygen mask first.

Your pain is there for a reason.

Fear and anxiety are normal in grief.

Finding ways to feel safe and comforted has to be a priority.

Dose your grief.

You need people.

Check in with yourself.

You are not in control of life.

Long-term denial harms you.

Being out-of-control in grief is normal.

Griefbursts are normal.

You're in the process of figuring things out for
yourself. It's a long process.

You're not failing at grief.

Your story of love and loss is precious. It needs to be told.

You have to go backward before you can go forward.

Tell the story. Tell the story. Tell the story.

You are a spiritual person. Lean into it.

There is value in the search for meaning.

It's important to learn to live with uncertainty.

Take time every day to care for your spiritual self.

Embrace mystical experiences.

Grief rituals can facilitate healing.

# Step Toward Truly Living
## Even as You Grieve

"I am filled with gratitude for this life I've received.
And I'm learning to look forward with hope, and live
in the present with an accepting and open heart."

In the early days after the death of someone you love dearly, it's
normal for this step to seem like a ridiculous impossibility. You
feel so raw and torn apart, you can't imagine surviving, let alone
returning to any semblance of "normal life."

But then the first couple of weeks pass, the funeral has been held,
and there it is—normal life, staring you in the face.

How can it be? You're still torn apart. You're still immersed in
shock and numbness. You're still shattered—completely crazed
by grief. But nonetheless, you have to keep getting out of bed and
walking the dog and paying the bills and trying to eat. It's crazy
making.

Life, as they say, goes on. It seems unbelievable, but it does. Your
inner world may have stopped, but the outer world has not. And
even your own life—with all its daily needs and responsibilities—
hasn't stopped either. So here you are, living while grieving.

But now I want to talk about *truly* living while grieving. That is, not just surviving but engaging with each day in life-affirming ways even as you continue to grieve and mourn.

If you're still in early survival mode, you might not be ready for this chapter. If so, it is perfectly OK at this point for you to tuck a bookmark into this page and set down the book for a while. As with all things in grief, you and only you get to decide if and when you're in a place to consider the ideas outlined here.

But if you feel like beginning to think about the longer term, let's keep going.

## Grief Is Forever

People often ask me how long grief lasts.

The hard truth is that grief is forever.

As long as you love the person who died, you will continue to grieve them. Because grief *is* love, grief doesn't discretely end.

But thank goodness, grief *does* change over time. It softens. The intense early pain grows duller then eventually settles into the background—especially if you've been actively mourning along the way. Like a serious but healed wound on your body, it's always there, but it no longer demands your daily (or hourly or minute-by-minute) attention. Nor does it hurt so much.

Love doesn't end. It learns to live with the absence.

I promise you, you will feel better. Your life will feel normal again, even though it will be a new normal.

# Grief and Truly Living Can Coexist

You've already learned that you have no choice but to keep living after a significant loss. You live even as you grieve.

True, in the beginning, that living is merely surviving. One day at a time, one second at a time. But as you begin to integrate the absence of the person who died, over time and through active mourning, your survival mode can start to move toward a truly-living mode.

Remember in Step 5 we talked about how to tell if an activity is a spiritual practice? I said that if something helps you do one or more of the following, then for you, it's a spiritual practice:

- Step away from judgment, control, worry, and conflict.

- Listen to your intuition.

- Experience renewal in solitude.

- Acknowledge the sacredness and privilege of being alive.

- Be your best self.

- Enjoy a sense of wellbeing.

- Feel at peace.

- Give and receive love.

- Feel gratitude and appreciation.

- Smile and laugh.

- Experience playfulness and levity.

- Feel a sense of meaning and purpose.

- Feel connected with others, the natural world, and, for some of you, your God or Source.

Now it is time to build awareness that the items on this same list are also characteristics of truly living. In other words, they are indicators of your quality of life.

When you are feeling gratitude and appreciation, for example, you're truly living. When you are giving and receiving love, you're truly living. When you are enjoying a sense of wellbeing and feeling meaning and purpose, you're truly living.

Truly living means being present to your life in ways that acknowledge the good and the beautiful. It means bringing your awareness to the opportunities for pleasure and joy that are available to you each day. It's an intentional way of embracing the moments—be they hours, days, months, or years—that are ahead of you.

## Everything Belongs

"I'm recognizing that there are people all around me, everywhere, who have also lost something irreplaceable. I've come to understand that if you live very long on this earth, you come to know loss. We are all in the same boat."

Of course, truly living also means being present to and fully engaging with the difficult experiences in life, including death and grief.

Love and attachment are indeed wonderful, but the circumstances of life are impermanent. No matter how devotedly we love and try to safeguard our attachments, things change.

People get sick. People age. People die. Pets too. People betray us. We betray ourselves. Passions ebb and flow. Fortunes rise and fall. And no matter what happens, the world just keeps turning.

Change is actually more of a constant than any stability we may experience.

Even though I do in fact think we're born to live and love, I also believe we can get better at acknowledging that loss is a big and unavoidable part of human life. Loss isn't really crazy. It's normal, too. Pretending that life is all roses isn't truly living—it's denial.

When bad things happen, there are three paths. One is denial. Another is permanent, all-pervasive grief and pessimism. And the third is experiencing and mourning the life losses even as you continue to truly live.

The human experience includes joys and hard work and challenges and heartbreaks in a crazy mixture. The third path is the one that acknowledges that everything belongs. Truly living means being open to and acknowledging all of it. It also means maintaining the belief that it's a privilege to live and love every precious day—even the grief-filled ones.

Some people come to grief and think their life is over. They are so torn apart and in so much pain that they cannot imagine their life will ever be good again. Have you felt this way? In the early days, it is completely understandable and normal. The grief and darkness take over, and for a time there is little more than pain and sorrow.

That's why Steps 1 through 5 are essential in early grief. You need them to survive your time of darkness. But eventually your grief work becomes developing the understanding that grieving and truly living are not mutually exclusive. You can do both at the same time. In fact, as I'll explain on p. 113, authentic mourning is yet another facet of truly living.

# Gaining Heart Understanding

Acknowledging the reality of the death is a central need in early grief. But in your early grief, you're just beginning to acknowledge the terrible truth with your head. In other words, you're facing and absorbing the reality cognitively—with your head, but not necessarily with your heart.

Yes, you understand that the person is no longer alive. Yes, you know what death means. But it takes much longer to gain heart understanding. Heart understanding is the deeper knowing of what the death will mean and feel like in your ongoing life. What are the death's many repercussions? What additional losses are you facing beyond the death itself?

For example, you may be losing hopes, goals, and dreams. You might lose financial security and experience dramatic changes in your daily routine and lifestyle. You are also losing parts of your self-identity.

How will all of this influence your life? What will the profound and forever absence of this precious person mean a month from now, a year from now, a decade from now? How will you survive, be changed by your loss, and go on living with meaning and purpose until you die?

As you continue to live in grief, you will slowly begin to move from head understanding to heart understanding. And as you gain ever-deeper heart understanding, you can also gain wisdom that helps you step toward fully living.

It's a crazy trade-off. Often, death wakes us up to what's really important. And as it does so, we have the opportunity to take positive action based on our new awareness.

# Authentic Mourning Is Truly Living

Grief is love, and love is life.

I'm sure you agree that love is essential to truly living. Well, the corollary is also true—truly grieving through active, open mourning is also essential to truly living.

In psychology there's this concept called congruency. It means acting on the outside in alignment with how you feel on the inside. It means speaking and behaving in accordance with your true feelings and values.

Congruency is a really good thing to pay attention to because it helps you feel right with yourself. When you're congruent, you're living your truth. You're being honest with yourself and others. You're in harmony inside and out.

The opposite of congruency is disconnection and disharmony. When you feel one way and act another, it feels wrong. It is like you are two separate people, and the person on the outside isn't doing the right thing. In fact, being incongruent makes a lot of people feel crazy their whole life long.

So, being open and honest on the outside about your inner grief is foundational to truly living. In other words, for you, active, authentic mourning is now an inextricable part of truly living.

# Taking Good Care of Yourself Is Truly Living

In Step 2, we touched on the importance of good self-care in grief. We said that moving your body and making sleep a priority are ways to soothe your natural fears and anxieties. More fundamentally, taking good care of your body is the foundation of truly living.

If you've ever taken a psychology class, you probably remember Abraham Maslow's Hierarchy of Needs. It's a pyramid depicting our needs as human beings, from the most basic to the most esoteric.

Self-actualization

Esteem

Love/belonging

Safety

Physiological

Maslow believed, and most other psychologists and philosophers have since concurred, that taking good care of ourselves on all levels of the pyramid is what brings the most fulfillment in life. We have to start at the bottom, though, and work our way up.

We have to start by meeting our physiological needs for food, water, shelter, and sleep. After that, we need to feel safe and secure. Only when our needs on the first two levels are met can we begin to focus on meeting our higher-level needs—for love, self-esteem, and ultimately self-actualization.

When have you been the happiest and most fulfilled in your life? Think about the times when you've felt loved, connected, strong, respected by others and yourself, and rising to the challenge to be your best self. In these moments, you were living toward the top of Maslow's pyramid.

The top of the pyramid is where truly living happens. The bottom of the pyramid is where survival happens.

Taking good care of yourself in grief starts at the bottom of the pyramid. These are the non-negotiables that we reviewed in Steps 1, 2, and 3. But as you begin to integrate your loss and move toward truly living even as you grieve, you start spending more time and attention on your upper-pyramid needs.

## Seeking More Love, Meaning, Awe, and Joy Is Truly Living

The top floors of Maslow's pyramid are where love, meaning, awe, and joy live.

While in early grief it's normal and necessary to focus on the foundational-level needs of survival (Steps 1, 2, and 3 in this book), in the longer run it's not at all crazy to think that even as you're grieving, you can also work on these higher-level experiences. In fact, grief lives on the top floors, too.

Remember, grief is love and relationships. It's also tied up in self-identity and self-esteem. And in its search for meaning, it's the need to know, understand, achieve growth, and reach toward fulfilling your potential.

All of these things are at the top of Maslow's Hierarchy. That makes grief a natural roommate in the upper levels and the penthouse.

So when you're ready, think about ways in which you can build more love, meaning, awe, and joy into your days.

Nurturing love can be accomplished with little things like:

- getting together with a friend for coffee
- sending a handwritten card to someone who is special to you

- saying yes when someone invites you out for dinner
- surprising someone with a gift
- simply giving a genuine compliment

More broadly, connection with others grows with the building blocks of proximity—being in the same room together, repetition—spending time together frequently, and quality time—doing things together that allow you to have fun but also share things that matter. Don't forget that talking about your loss with your loved ones is also part of nurturing love.

Adding more meaning to your days is as simple as asking yourself, "What are some ways of spending time that feel meaningful to me?" Here are some self-care activities that can feel meaningful:

- taking a walk outdoors
- gardening
- cooking
- making art
- taking a class
- learning a new skill
- volunteering
- helping a neighbor or family member

And if you find meaning in certain loss-focused activities—such as volunteering for a cause related to the death or reaching out to someone else grieving the same loss—that counts, too. As always, you get to decide.

I think building the feeling of awe and wonder into your routines takes a little more thought—but it's more than worth it. Awe is that expansive feeling you get when you stand near the edge of the Grand Canyon, look at starry night sky, hold a newborn baby, or listen to an incredible musician. It's almost unbelievable that the world contains such amazing things.

Studies show that awe-filled moments boost your mood, improve your physical health, help you think more critically, foster generosity, and help you feel more connected to other people and humanity. So thinking about what makes you feel awe and adding some awe to your daily routine—even if it's through something as simple as spending time outdoors or watching YouTube nature videos—is a lovely way of improving your quality of life.

Finally, you need and deserve joy. Please don't forget that. Again, if you're not ready to seek joy, it's OK. You get to decide when the time is right. But when you are ready to welcome even some tiny morsels of joy into your time of grief, allow yourself the experience. It's not uncommon for grieving people to experience some of what I refer to as the "joy-guilt" syndrome. This is where you have a moment of joy but then feel feel a twinge of guilt about being happy. "How can I be happy when they're not here?" you might think. However, the real work at hand is allowing yourself to continue to mourn and know that experiencing all emotions—including joy—is a part of being able to eventually embrace meaning and purpose in your continued living.

Everything belongs, including guilt, sadness, and joy—all at the same time!

## The More You Truly Live, the More Life and Love You'll Experience

I realize that losing someone you love is beyond shattering. I'm sure that some of you reading this book have endured multiple significant and even traumatic losses. I honor your truth, and I extend you my deepest and most sincere empathy.

But even though change and loss are unavoidable, painful, and even overwhelming, we are here. And I believe that truly living is the best way we can choose to inhabit our time here on earth. Loving as well as its conjoined twin, grieving, are truly a privilege.

I sometimes think of this privilege in relation to the person who died as well. They are no longer here to enjoy life on earth. We miss them desperately. But what honors them more—stepping away from truly living and toward permanent grief? Or, stepping toward truly living and mourning at the same time?

Not only is truly living a responsibility, it's an opportunity. Every day offers us chances to experience miracles big and small. We can open ourselves to those miracles even as we continue to grieve. We can give and receive love. We can spend time in and marvel at nature. We can smile and laugh. We can help other people. We can experience connection. We can pursue meaning and purpose. We can feel joy and awe.

And when the next loss comes along, which it will, we can choose to keep truly mourning and truly living.

When you emerge from your early grief into the lifelong journey of living without the person who died, the choice is yours. You get to decide.

You can choose to truly live and grieve at the same time. Truly loving, truly grieving, truly living. They're all part and parcel of the best opportunities available to us as human beings.

You are here but a short time. I hope you'll choose to make the most of it.

## Reset Your Intention

It's time to revisit your grief intentions—those having to do with your emotional, social, and spiritual health.

Today I intend to: _____

_____

_____

_____

_____

This week I intend to: _____

_____

_____

_____

_____

This year I intend to: _____

_____

_____

_____

_____

In my future life, I intend to: _____

_____

_____

_____

_____

## THINGS TO REMEMBER

In grief, crazy is normal.

Grief is love.

Mourning helps you heal.

Grief and hope belong together.

There are no rewards for speed.

You get to decide.

Each grief is unique. Respect that.

Early symptoms of grief are necessary and normal.

Put on your own oxygen mask first.

Your pain is there for a reason.

Fear and anxiety are normal in grief.

Finding ways to feel safe and comforted has to be a priority.

Dose your grief.

You need people.

Check in with yourself.

You are not in control of life.

Long-term denial harms you.

Being out-of-control in grief is normal.

Griefbursts are normal.

You're in the process of figuring things out for
yourself. It's a long process.

You're not failing at grief.

Your story of love and loss is precious. It needs to be told.

You have to go backward before you can go forward.

Tell the story. Tell the story. Tell the story.

You are a spiritual person. Lean into it.

There is value in the search for meaning.

It's important to learn to live with uncertainty.

Take time every day to care for your spiritual self.

Embrace mystical experiences.

Grief rituals can facilitate healing.

Grief is forever.

Everything belongs.

Loss is normal, too.

Grief lives on the top floors.

You deserve love, meaning, awe, and joy.

# A Final Word

You're not crazy—you're grieving.

And you're understandably shattered—which *is* crazy in the truest sense of the word.

It is OK to feel crazy in grief. In fact, it's empowering to own your crazy.

The six steps introduced in this book will help you survive your early grief. I encourage you to turn to them again and again, whenever you find yourself struggling or in need of affirmation.

It is so hard being human. It is so painful to love and lose. But at the same time, it's also the greatest privilege I know of.

As I was wrapping up my writing on this book, I realized that in English we also use the word "crazy" to mean love.

"I'm crazy about you," we say.

Or: "I love _____ like crazy."

In this sense, the people and things we go crazy for are our passions. They are what give our lives meaning and purpose.

When you are feeling crazy about something, it means you care about it deeply. This kind of crazy is how you know you are alive.

So, as you step toward truly living even as you grieve, I urge you to remember to honor and follow your crazy.

Grieve like crazy.

Mourn like crazy.

Love like crazy.

Live like crazy.

I hope we meet one day.

# Companioning Versus Treating

To help you feel empowered to be in charge of your own grief, please allow me to introduce you to my grief counseling philosophy, which I call "companioning."

The word "treat" comes from the Latin root word *tractare*, which means "to drag." If we combine that with the word "patient," we can really get in trouble. "Patient" means passive long-term sufferer." So if as a grief counselor I treat patients, I drag passive long-term sufferers.

On the other hand, the word "companion," when broken down into its original Latin roots means "messmate": *com* for "with" and *pan* for "bread." Someone you would share a meal with, a friend, an equal. I have taken liberties with the noun "companion" and made it into the verb "companioning" because it so well captures the type of counseling relationship I support and advocate.

More specifically, grief counselors who embrace the companioning model understand that:

- Companioning is about being present to another person's pain; it is not about taking away the pain.

- Companioning is about going to the wilderness of the soul with another human being; it is not about thinking you are responsible for finding the way out.

- Companioning is about honoring the spirit; it is not about focusing on the intellect.

- Companioning is about listening with the heart; it is not about analyzing with the head.

- Companioning is about bearing witness to the struggles of others; it is not about judging or directing these struggles.

- Companioning is about walking alongside; it is not about leading.

- Companioning is about discovering the gifts of sacred silence; it is not about filling up every moment with words.

- Companioning is about being still; it is not about frantic movement forward.

- Companioning is about respecting disorder and confusion; it is not about imposing order and logic.

- Companioning is about learning from others; it is not about teaching them.

- Companioning is about compassionate curiosity; it is not about expertise.

I always invite—and sometimes even challenge—caregivers who come to my trainings at the Center for Loss to adopt a companioning, teach-me attitude with people in grief. When we think of ourselves as grief companions, we are less likely to make inappropriate interpretations or judgments of the mourner's experiences. This approach helps ensure that when a person in grief expresses thoughts, feelings, or attitudes, we consciously avoid making evaluative responses. Reactions such as, "That's right or wrong," "That shouldn't be," or worse yet, "That's pathological" are anchored in judgments that are inappropriate and often damaging. Instead, all responses are valid, and everything belongs.

# The Six Needs of Mourning

While the six steps are for surviving early grief, the following six reconciliation needs of mourning will help you continue your healing momentum. You will notice many echoes of the six steps in the six needs.

For a more in-depth exploration of the six needs of mourning as well as other principles of grief, mourning, and healing, I invite you to read my book *Understanding Your Grief: Ten Essential Touchstones for Finding Hope and Healing Your Heart*.

### MOURNING NEED 1: Acknowledge the reality of the death

When we are in grief, we have a need to fully acknowledge the reality of the death. We do this not only with our heads, but also with our hearts. Encountering this reality is challenging, to say the least, but also essential.

### MOURNING NEED 2: Embrace the pain of the loss

Grief is necessary, and so is the pain of grief. This need asks you to acknowledge the appropriateness of your pain as well as learn to look upon your pain as part of your love for the person who died. If love is good and valuable, so, too, is grief. And like love, grief will require your loving attention throughout the years to come.

### MOURNING NEED 3: Remember the person who died

On the grief journey, we convert our relationship with the person who died from one of presence to one of memory. I often say, "You must listen to the music of the past, so you can sing in the present, and dance into the future." Healing in grief requires ongoing remembering and cherishing of the person who died.

**MOURNING NEED 4: Develop a new self-identity**

After someone central to our lives dies, we are different. The ways in which we think of our lives and ourselves changes. In addition, sometimes the way society views us is impacted. Our daily routines may change. Our passions and purpose evolve. Our ongoing grief calls for us to continue to work on considering and re-defining our self-identities.

**MOURNING NEED 5: Search for meaning**

We naturally wonder about the "whys" of life and death when we are in grief. What is the purpose of life? Why are we here? Why did someone we love have to die, now and in this way? Why go on? These are the kinds of questions we wrestle with in our hearts and souls. We may also struggle with our belief systems. Grief is a spiritual journey, and this mourning need arises because our spirits are wounded. Our ongoing grief requires us to continue to actively ponder the meaning of life in general and the meaning of our continuing, individual lives in particular.

**MOURNING NEED 6: Receive and accept help from others**

Since mourning is expressing our grief outside ourselves, healing in grief is in part a social process. We need and deserve the empathy and support of others as we actively encounter and share our grief.

## About the Author

Alan D. Wolfelt, Ph.D., is a respected author and educator on the topics of companioning others and healing in grief. He serves as Director of the Center for Loss and Life Transition and is on the faculty at the University of Colorado Medical School's Department of Family Medicine. Dr. Wolfelt has written many bestselling books on healing in grief, including *Understanding*

 *Your Grief, Healing Your Grieving Heart*, and *Grief One Day at a Time*. Visit www. centerforloss.com to learn more about grief and loss and to order Dr. Wolfelt's books.

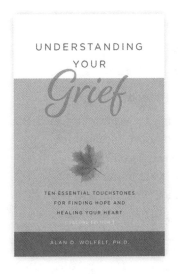

# Understanding Your Grief

Since its debut in 1992, this favorite by one of the world's most beloved grief counselors has found a place in the homes and hearts of hundreds of thousands of mourners across the globe. Filled with compassion and hope, *Understanding Your Grief* helps you understand and befriend your painful, complex, yet normal thoughts and feelings after the death of someone loved.

*Understanding Your Grief* is built on Dr. Wolfelt's Ten Touchstones—basic principles to learn and actions to take to help yourself engage with your grief and create momentum toward healing. This second edition includes concise additional wisdom on new topics such as the myth of closure, complicated and traumatic grief, grief overload, loneliness, the power of ritual, and more. Excellent as an empathetic handbook for anyone in mourning as well as a text for support groups, *Understanding Your Grief* also pairs with *The Understanding Your Grief Journal*.

If you're grieving a death or a significant loss of any kind, this refreshed bestseller will be your rock and steadfast companion as you journey through the wilderness of your unique grief.

ISBN 978-1-61722-307-5 • 215 pages • softcover • $14.95

ALL DR. WOLFELT'S PUBLICATIONS CAN BE ORDERED BY MAIL FROM:

Companion Press | 3735 Broken Bow Road | Fort Collins, CO 80526
(970) 226-6050 | www.centerforloss.com

# ALSO BY ALAN WOLFELT

## Grief One Day at a Time: 365 Meditations to Help You Heal After Loss

After someone you love dies, each day can be a struggle. But each day, you can also find comfort and understanding in this daily companion. With one brief entry for every day of the calendar year, this little book offers small, one-day-at-a-time doses of guidance and healing. Each entry includes an inspiring or soothing quote followed by a short discussion of the day's theme. How do you get through the loss of a loved one? One day at a time. This compassionate gem of a book will accompany you.

"**Each day I look forward to reading a new page...I can't imagine dealing with my sorrow without [this] book.**"

— A reader

ISBN 978-1-61722-238-2 • 384 pages • softcover • $14.95

ALL DR. WOLFELT'S PUBLICATIONS CAN BE ORDERED BY MAIL FROM:

Companion Press | 3735 Broken Bow Road | Fort Collins, CO 80526
(970) 226-6050 | www.centerforloss.com